THE *Lyric* Li...

Pop/Rock Ballads

Complete Lyrics for 200 Songs

DISCARD

HAL•LEONARD®

Other books in *The Lyric Library*:

Broadway Volume I
Broadway Volume II
Christmas
Classic Rock
Contemporary Christian
Country
Early Rock 'n' Roll
Love Songs

ISBN 0-634-04476-1

Library of Congress cataloguing-in-publication data has been applied for.

Visit Hal Leonard Online at
www.halleonard.com

Preface

Songs have an uncanny ability to burrow deep into our gray matter, sometimes lying dormant for years or decades before something pings them back into our consciousness. All kinds of songs reside in there, more than we can count—not just songs we love and intentionally memorized and have sung again and again, but songs we once heard in passing, songs that form a soundtrack to significant people and places and moments in our lives, and even (or especially) songs that drive us crazy, like the chirping TV jingle that still won't let go years after the product it plugged has disappeared from the shelves.

Most of the time, though, our memories of songs are frustratingly incomplete unless we actively maintain them. The first verse and chorus that we blare out in the shower or at the jam session degenerates into mumbled lines, disconnected phrases, and bits and pieces inadvertently lifted from other songs. And, of course, there's the likelihood that what we *do* remember is riddled with mondegreens, or misheard lyrics. In these pages you'll find many opportunities to bring a little more completeness and accuracy to your repertoire of pop ballads, as well as to rediscover a nearly forgotten gem, wallow in nostalgia, or just browse through some prominent examples of the songwriter's craft.

Originally, ballads were primarily a storytelling vehicle, with repetitive, rhythmic forms and long (sometimes very long) strings of verses spinning out dramatic or bawdy tales that were passed along, embellished, and altered over the years. This was the tradition brought to America by many waves of European immigrants and then tapped by balladeers like Woody Guthrie, though it remains largely dormant in our era as "ballad" has come to mean essentially a slow and often reflective song (in songwriting lingo, the closest thing to the old meaning of "ballad" would be "story song"). In pop/rock, ballads are the stock-in-trade of what's become known as soft rock; on the harder-rocking end of the spectrum, ballads provide a mellow contrast to the crunching guitars and propulsive beats.

When the music speaks to us more gently and quietly, we tend to lean in and pay closer attention to the lyrics. And songwriters rise to the occasion with their most emotionally intimate and achingly personal expressions, killing us softly with their songs.

Contents

Pop/Rock Ballads

Adia

Words and Music by Sarah McLachlan and Pierre Marchand

recorded by Sarah McLachlan

Adia, I do believe I failed you.
Adia, I know I've let you down.
Don't you know I tried so hard,
To love you in my way;
It's easy, let it go.

Adia, I'm empty since you left me.
Trying to find a way to carry on;
I search myself and everyone,
To see where we went wrong.
There's no one left to finger,
There's no on here to blame.
There's no one left to talk to honey,
And there ain't no one to buy
    our innocence;
'Cause we are born innocent.
Believe me, Adia,
We are still innocent.
It's easy, we all falter.
And does it matter?

Adia, I thought that we could make it.
I know I can't change the way you feel.
I leave you with your misery,
A friend who won't betray.
Pull you from your tower,
I take a away your pain.
I show you all the beauty you possess.
If you'd only let yourself believe,
That we are born innocent.
It's easy, we all falter.
And does it matter?

'Cause we are born innocent.
Believe me, Adia,
We are still innocent.
It's easy, we all falter,
Does it matter?
Believe me, Adia,
We are still innocent.
'Cause we are born innocent.
Believe me, Adia,
We are still innocent.
Its easy, we all falter,
Does it matter?

After the Love Has Gone

Words and Music by David Foster, Jay Graydon and Bill Champlin

recorded by Earth, Wind & Fire

For a while to love was all we could do;
We were young and we knew,
And our eyes were alive.
Deep inside we knew our love was true.
For awhile we paid no mind to the past,
We knew love would last.
Every night
Somethin' right
Would invite us to begin the dance.

Somethin' happened along the way;
What used to be happy was sad.
Somethin' happened along the way
And yesterday was all we had.

Oh, after the love has gone,
How could you lead me on,
And not let me stay around?
Oh, after the love has gone,
What used to be right is wrong.
Can love that's lost be found?

For awhile,
To love each other was all we would
    ever need.
Love was strong for so long,
Never knew that what was wrong,
Baby, wasn't right.
We tried to find what we had
'Til sadness was all we shared.
We were scared this affair
Would lead our love into...

Somethin' happened along the way;
Yesterday was all we had.
Somethin' happened along the way;
What used to be happy is sad.
Somethin' happened along the way;
What used to be was all we had.
Oh, after the love has gone,
How could you lead me on
And not let me stay around?

Oh, after the love has gone,
What used to be right is wrong.
Can love that's lost be found?

Oh, after the love has gone,
What used to be right is wrong.
Can love that's lost be found?

Against All Odds (Take a Look at Me Now)

Words and Music by Phil Collins

from the film *Against All Odds*
recorded by Phil Collins

How can I just let you walk away,
Just let you leave without a trace?
When I stand here taking
Every breath with you,
You're the only one
Who really knows me at all.
How can you just walk away from me,
When all I can do is watch you leave.
'Cause we've shared the laughter and
  the pain,
And even shared the tears.
You're the only one who really knew
  me at all.

So take a look at me now
'Cause there's just an empty space.
There's nothing left here to remind me,
Just the memory of your face.
So take a look at me now,
There's just an empty space,
And you coming back to me is against
  the odds,
And that's what I've got to face.

I wish I could just make you turn around,
Turn around and see me cry.
There's so much I need to say to you,
So many reasons why
You're the only one who really knew
  me at all.

So take a look at me now,
There's just an empty space,
And there's nothing left here to remind me,
Just the memory of your face.
So take a look at me now,
'Cause there's just an empty space.
But to wait for you is all I can do,
And that's what I've got to face.

Take a good look at me now
'Cause I'll still be standing here,
And you coming back to me is against
  all odds.
That's the chance I've got to take...
Take a look at me now.

The Air That I Breathe

Words and Music by Albert Hammond and Michael Hazelwood

recorded by The Hollies

If I could make a wish I think I'd pass,
Can't think of anything I need.
No cigarettes, no sleep, no light, no sound,
Nothing to eat, no books to read.

Making love with you
Has left me peaceful, warm and tired.
What more could I ask,
There's nothing left to be desired.

Peace came upon me and it leaves me weak.
Sleep, silent angel, go to sleep.

Sometimes,
All I need is the air that I breathe.
And to love you,
All I need is the air that breathe.
Yes, to love you,
All I need is the air that I breathe.

Peace came upon me and it leaves me weak.
Sleep, silent angel, go to sleep.

All for Love

Words and Music by Bryan Adams, Robert John "Mutt" Lange and Michael Kamen

from Walt Disney Pictures' *The Three Musketeers*
recorded by Bryan Adams, Sting & Rod Stewart

When it's love you give
(I'll be a man of good faith.)
Then in love you'll live.
(I'll make a stand. I won't break.)
I'll be the rock you can build on,
Be there when you're old,
To have and to hold.
When there's love inside pain.

(I swear I'll always be strong.)
Then there's a reason why.
(I'll prove to you we belong.)
I'll be the wall that protects you
From the wind and the rain,
From the hurt and pain.

Refrain:
Let's make it all for one and all for love.
Let the one you hold be the one you want,
The one you need,
'Cause it's all for the one for all.
When there's someone that should know,
Then just let your feelings show,
And make it all for one and all for love.

Then it's love you make.
(I'll be the fire in your night.)
Then it's love you take.
(I will defend, I will fight.)
I'll be there when you need me.
When honor's at stake,
This vow I will make:

Refrain

Don't lay our love to rest
'Cause we could stand up to the test.
We got everything and more than we had
    planned,
More than the rivers that run the land.
We got it all in our hands.

Now it's all for one and all for love.
(It's all for love.)
Let the one you hold be the one you want,
The one you need.
'Cause when it's all for one it's one for all.
(It's one for all.)
When there's someone that should know,
Then just let your feelings show.
When there's someone that you want,
When there's someone that you need,
Let's make it all, all for one,
And all for love.

All in Love Is Fair

Words and Music by Stevie Wonder

recorded by Stevie Wonder

All is fair in love.
Love's a crazy game.
Two people vow to stay
In love as one they say
But all is changed with time.
The future none can see.
The road you leave behind.
Ahead lies mystery,
But all is fair in love.
I had to go away.
A writer takes his pen,
To write the words again,
That all in love is fair.

All of fate's a chance.
It's either good or bad.
I tossed my coin to say,
In love with me you'd stay,
But all in war is cold.
You either win or lose.
When all is put away,
The losing side I'll play.
But all is fair in love.
I should never have left your side.
A writer takes his pen,
To write the words again,
That all in love is fair.

A writer takes his pen,
To write the words again,
That all in love is fair.

All My Life

Words by Joel Hailey
Music by Joel Hailey and Rory Bennett

recorded by K-Ci & JoJo

Baby, baby, baby, baby, baby,
Baby, baby, baby, baby, baby, babe.

I will never find another lover sweeter
   than you,
Sweeter than you.
And I will never find another lover more
   preious than you,
More precious than you.
Girl, you are close to me,
You're like my mother,
Close to me,
You're like my father,
Close to me,
You're like my sister,
Close to me,
You're like my brother.
You are the only one.
You're my everything
And for you this song I sing.

Refrain:
And all my life
I prayed for someone like you,
And I thank God that I,
That I finally found you.
For all my life
I prayed for someone like you,
And I hope that you
Feel the same way too.
Yes, I pray that you
Do love me too.

I said that you're all that I'm thinking of.
Da, da, da...
Said I promise to never fall in love with a
   stranger.
You're all I'm thinking of.
I praise the Lord above
For sending me your love.

I cherish every hug.
I really love you.
For...

Refrain

You're all that I ever know.
When you smile on my face,
All I see is a glow.
You turned my life around.
You picked me up when I was down.
You're all that I ever know.

When you smile life is glow.
You picked me up when I was down.
Sayin' you're all that I ever know.
When you smile life is glow.
You picked me up when I was down.
And I hope that you
Feel the same way too.

Repeat Refrain and Fade

All Out of Love

Words and Music by Graham Russell and Clive Davis

Recorded by Air Supply

I'm lying alone with my head on the phone,
Thinking of you 'til it hurts.
I know you hurt too, but what else can we do,
Tormented and torn apart.

I wish I could carry your smile in my heart,
For times when my life feels so low.
It would make me believe what tomorrow could bring,
When today doesn't really know, doesn't really know.

Refrain:
I'm all out of love, I'm so lost without you,
I know you were right, believing for so long.
I'm all out of love, what am I without you?
I can't be too late to say that I was so wrong.

I want you to come back and carry me home,
Away from these long, lonely nights.
I'm reaching for you. Are you feeling it too?
Does the feeling seem oh, so right?

And what would you say if I called on you now,
And said that I can't hold on?
There's no easy way, it gets harder each day,
Please love me or I'll be gone, I'll be gone.

Refrain

Ooh, what are you thinking of?
What are you thinking of?
What are you thinking of?
What are you thinking of?

Refrain

Almost Paradise

Words by Dean Pitchford
Music by Eric Carmen

Love Theme from the Paramount Motion Picture *Footloose*
from the Broadway Musical *Footloose*
recorded by Mike Reno & Ann Wilson

Ren:
I thought that dreams belonged
   to other men,
'Cause each time I got close,
   they'd fall apart again.

Ariel:
I feared my heart would beat in secrecy.

Both:
I faced the nights alone.
Oh, how could I have known
That all my life I only needed you?

Refrain:
Whoa, almost paradise,
We're knockin' on heaven's door.
Almost paradise,
How could we ask for more?
I swear that I can see forever in your eyes.
Paradise.

Ariel:
I thought that perfect love was
   hard to find.
I'd almost given up; you must have
   read my mind.

Ren:
And all those dreams I saved for a rainy day,

Ariel:
Ooh, they're fin'lly coming true.
I'll share them all with you,
'Cause now we hold the future in our hands.

Refrain

Ren:
And in your arms salvation's not so far away.

Ariel:
It's getting closer, closer ev'ry day.

Refrain

Paradise.
Paradise.

Alone

Words and Music by Billy Steinberg and Tom Kelly

recorded by Heart

I hear the ticking of the clock;
I'm lying here, the room's pitch dark.
I wonder where you are tonight,
No answer on the telephone.
And the night goes by so very slow,
Oh, I hope that it won't end, though,
Alone.

Refrain:
'Til now I always got by on my own,
I never really cared until I met you.
And now it chills me to the bone.
How do I get you alone?
How do I get you alone?

You don't know how long I have wanted
To touch your lips and hold you tight.
You don't know how long I have waited,
And I was gonna tell you tonight.
But the secret is still my own,
And my love for you is still unknown,
Alone.

Refrain

How do I get you alone?
How do I get you alone,
Alone, alone?

Always on My Mind

Words and Music by Wayne Thompson, Mark James and Johnny Christopher

recorded by Willie Nelson, The Pet Shop Boys, Elvis Presley

Maybe I didn't treat you
Quite as good as I should have.
Maybe I didn't love you,
Quite as often as I should have;
Little things I should have said and done,
I just never took the time.

You were always on my mind;
You were always on my mind.

Tell me,
Tell me that your sweet love hasn't died.
Give me,
Give me one more chance to keep you satisfied, satisfied.

Maybe I didn't hold you,
All those lonely, lonely times;
And I guess I never told you
I'm so happy that you're mine.
If I made you feel second best,
Girl, I'm sorry I was blind.

You were always on my mind;
You were always on my mind.

Amazed

Words and Music by Marv Green, Chris Lindsey and Aimee Mayo

recorded by Lonestar

Every time our eyes meet,
This feelin' inside me
Is almost more than I can take.
Baby, when you touch me,
I can feel how much you love me,
And it just blows me away.
I've never been this close to anyone
   or anything.
I can hear your thoughts.
I can see your dreams.

Refrain:
I don't know how you do what you do,
I'm so in love with you.
It just keeps gettin' better.
I wanna spend the rest of my life
With you by my side, forever and ever.
Every little thing that you do,
Baby, I'm amazed by you.

The smell of your skin,
The taste of your kiss,
The way you whisper in the dark.
Your hair all around me;
Baby, you surround me.
You touch every place in my heart.
Oh, it feels like the first time every time.
I wanna spend the whole night in your eyes.

Refrain

Every little thing that you do
I'm so in love with you.
It just keeps gettin' better.
I wanna spend the rest of my life
With you by my side forever and ever.
Every little thing that you do,
Oh, every little thing that you do,
Baby, I'm amazed by you.

And So It Goes

Words and Music by Billy Joel

recorded by Billy Joel

In every heart there is a room,
A sanctuary safe and strong.
To heal the wounds from lovers past,
Until a new one comes along.
I spoke to you in cautious tones;
You answered me with no pretense.
And still I feel I said too much.
My silence is a defense.

And every time I've held a rose,
It seems I only felt the thorns.
And so it goes.
And so it goes.
And so will you soon I suppose.
But if my silence made you leave,
Then that would be my worst mistake.
So I will share this room with you,
And you can have this heart to break.

And this is why my eyes are closed,
It's just as well for all I've seen.
And so it goes.
And so it goes.
And you're the only one who knows.

So I would choose to be with you.
That's if the choice were mine to make.
But you can make decisions too.
And you can have this heart to break.
And so it goes
And so it goes
And you're the only one who knows.

Angel

Words and Music by Sarah McLachlan

recorded by Sarah McLachlan

Spend all your time waiting
For that second chance,
For a break that would make it okay.
There's always some reason
To feel not good enough,
And it's hard at the end of the day.
I need some distraction oh,
   beautiful release.
Memory seep from my veins.
Let me be empty,
Oh, and weightless and maybe
I'll find some peace tonight

In the arms of the angel.
Fly away from here,
From this dark, cold hotel room,
And the endlessness that you fear.
You are pulled from the wreckage
Of your silent reverie.
You're in the arms of the angel.
May you find some comfort here.

You're so tired of the straight line,
And everywhere you turn
There's vultures and thieves at your back.
Storm keeps on twisting.
Keep on building the lies,
And you make up for all that you lack.
It don't make no difference
Escaping one last time.
It's easier to believe
In this sweet madness,
Oh, this glorious sadness
That brings me to my knees

In the arms of the angel.
Fly away from here,
From this dark, cold hotel room
And the endlessness that you fear.
You are pulled from the wreckage
Of your silent reverie.
You're in the arms of the angel.
May you find some comfort here.

Annie's Song

Words and Music by John Denver

recorded by John Denver

You fill up my senses,
Like a night in a forest,
Like the mountains in springtime,
Like a walk in the rain.
Like a storm in the desert,
Like a sleepy blue ocean.
You fill up my senses,
Come fill me again.

Come let me love you,
Let me give my life to you,
Let me drown in your laughter,
Let me die in your arms.
Let me lay down beside you,
Let me always be with you,
Come let me love you,
Come love me again.

Repeat Verse 1

At Seventeen

Words and Music by Janis Ian

recorded by Janis Ian

I learned the truth at seventeen;
That love was meant for beauty queens,
And high school girls with clear-skinned
    smiles,
Who married young and then retired.
The valentines I never knew,
The Friday night charades of youth,
Were spent on one more beautiful;
At seventeen, I learned the truth.

And those of us with ravaged faces,
Lacking in the social graces,
Desperately remained at home.
Inventing lovers on the phone,
Who called to say, "Come dance with me,"
And murmured vague obscenities.
It isn't all it seems
At seventeen.

A brown-eyed girl in hand-me-downs,
Whose name I never could pronounce,
Said, "Pity, please, the ones who serve.
They only get what they deserve.
The rich-relationed home town queen
Marries into what she needs,
A guarantee of company
And haven for the elderly."

Remember those who win the game,
Lose the love they sought to gain,
In debentures of quality,
And dubious integrity.
Their small town eyes will gape at you,
In dull surprise when payment due
Exceeds accounts received
At seventeen.

To those of us who know the pain
Of valentines that never came,
And those whose names were never called,
When choosing sides for basketball.
It was long ago and far away.
The world was younger than today,
And dreams were all they gave for free,
To ugly duckling girls like me.

We all play the game and when we dare
To cheat ourselves at solitaire,
Inventing lovers on the phone,
Repenting other lives unknown,
That call and say, "Come dance with me,"
And murmur vague obscenities,
At ugly girls like me;
At seventeen.

Baby What a Big Surprise

Words and Music by Peter Cetera

recorded by Chicago

Right before my very eyes,
I thought that you were only fakin' it,
And like before my heart was takin' it.
Baby, what a big surprise;
Right before my very eyes, oh, oh, oh.

Yesterday it seemed to me
My life was nothing more than wasted time.
But here today you softly changed my mind.
Baby, what a big surprise;
Right before my very eyes, oh, oh, oh.

Just to be alone was a little more than I could take,
Then you came to stay. Oo..
Hold me in the morning, love me in the afternoon.
Help me find my way, hey, yeah.
Now and then just like before
I think about the love I've thrown away,
But now it doesn't matter anyway.

Repeat and Fade:
Baby, what a big surprise;
Right before my very eyes, oh, oh, oh.

Baby, I'm-A Want You

Words and Music by David Gates

recorded by Bread

Baby, I'm a-want you.
Baby, I'm a-need you.
You the only one I care enough to hurt about.
Maybe I'm a-crazy, but I just can't live without
Your lovin' and affection, givin' me direction,
Like a guiding light to help me through my darkest hour.
Lately I'm a-prayin' that you'll always be a-stayin' beside me.

Used to be my life was just emotions passing by,
Feeling all the while and never really knowing why.

Lately I'm a-prayin' that you'll always be a-stayin' beside me.

Used to be my life was just emotions passing by.
Then you came along and made me laugh and made me cry.
You taught me why.

Baby, I'm a-want you.
Baby, I'm a-need you.
Oh, it took so long to find you, baby.
Baby, I'm a-want you.
Baby, I'm a-need you.

Beauty and the Beast

Lyrics by Howard Ashman
Music by Alan Menken

from Walt Disney's *Beauty and the Beast*
recorded by Celine Dion & Peabo Bryson

Tale as old as time,
True as it can be.
Barely even friends,
Then somebody bends
Unexpectedly.

Just a little change.
Small, to say the least.
Both a little scared,
Neither one prepared.
Beauty and the Beast.
Ever just the same.
Ever a surprise.
Ever as before,
Ever just as sure
As the sun will rise.

Tale as old as time.
Tune as old as song.
Bittersweet and strange,
Finding you can change,
Learning you were wrong.

Certain as the sun
Rising in the East.
Tale as old as time,
Song as old as rhyme.
Beauty and the Beast.

Tale as old as time,
Song as old as rhyme
Beauty and the Beast.

Bein' Green

Words and Music by Joe Raposo

from the television show *Sesame Street*

It's not that easy bein' green,
Having to spend each day the color of the leaves.
When I think it could be nicer bein' red or yellow or gold,
Or something much more colorful like that.

It's not easy bein' green,
It seems you blend in with so many other ordinary things,
And people tend to pass you over, 'cause you're not standing out
Like flashy sparkles on the water or stars in the sky.

But green is the color of spring,
And green can be cool and friendly like.
And green can be big like an ocean,
Or important like a mountain or tall like a tree.

When green is all there is to be,
It could make you wonder why,
But why wonder, why wonder?
I am green and it'll do fine,
It's beautiful, and I think it's what I want to be.

Ben

Words by Don Black
Music by Walter Scharf

from the film *Ben*
recorded by Michael Jackson

Ben, the two of us need look no more,
We both found what we were looking for.
With a friend to call my own,
I'll never be alone,
And you my friend will see,
You've got a friend in me.

Ben, you're always running here and there,
You feel you're not wanted anywhere.
If you ever look behind,
And don't like what you find,
There's something you should know,
You've got a place to go.

I used to say I and me,
Now it's us, now it's we.
I used to say I and me,
Now it's us, now its we.
Ben, most people would turn you away,
I don't listen to a word they say.
They don't see you as I do,
I wish they would try to.
I'm sure they'd think again if they had a friend like Ben

Like Ben, like Ben, like Ben, like Ben.

Best of My Love

Words and Music by John David Souther, Don Henley and Glenn Frey

recorded by The Eagles

Every night
I'm lying in bed,
Holdin' you close in my dreams;
Thinkin' about all the things that we said
And comin' apart at the seams.
We try to talk it over
But the words come out too rough;
I know you were tryin'
To give me the best of your love.

Beautiful faces,
Loud empty places
Look at the way that we live,
Wastin' our time
On cheap talk and wine
Left us so little to give.

The same old crowd
Was like a cold dark cloud
That we could never rise above,
But here in my heart
I give you the best of my love.

Oh, sweet darlin',
You get the best of my love,
(You get the best of my love.)
Oh, sweet darlin',
You get the best of my love.
(You get the best of my love.)

I'm goin' back in time
And it's a sweet dream.
It was a quiet night
And I would be alright
If I could go on sleeping.

But every mornin'
I wake up and worry
What's gonna happen today.
You see it your way,
And I see it mine,
But we both see it slippin' away.

You know, we always had each other, baby.
I guess that wasn't enough.
Oh, but here in my heart
I give you the best of my love.
Oh, sweet darlin',
You get the best of my love.
Oh, sweet darlin',
You get the best of my love.

Biggest Part of Me

Words and Music by David Pack

recorded by Ambrosia

(Sunrise) There's a new sun arisin'.
(In your eyes) I can see a new horizon
(Realize) That will keep me realizin'
You're the biggest part of me.
(Stay the night) Need your lovin' here
  beside me.
(Shine the light) Need you close enough
  to guide me.
(For all my life) I've been hopin' you
  would find me.
You're the biggest part of me.

Refrain:
Make a wish, baby.
Well, and I will make it come true.
Make a list, baby,
Of the things I'll do for you.
Ain't no risk, now,
In lettin' my love rain down on you,
So we could wash away the past,
So that we may start anew.

(Rainbow) Risin' over my shoulder;
(Love flows) Gettin' better as we're older.
(All I know) All I want to do is hold her.
She's the life that breathes in me.
(Forever) Got a feelin' that forever.
(Together) We are gonna stay together.
(For better) For me, there's nothing better.
You're biggest part of me.

Refrain

More than an easy feelin',
She brings joy to me.
How can I tell you
What it means to me?
Flow like a lazy river
For an eternity.
I've fin'lly found someone
Who believes in me,
And I'll never leave.

(Beside me) Need your lovin' here
  beside me.
(To guide me) Keep it close enough
  to guide me.
(Inside of me) From the fears that are
  inside of me.
You're the biggest part of me.
(Forever) Got a feelin' that forever
(Together) We are gonna stay together
(Forever) From now until forever.
You're the biggest part of me.
You're the life that breathes in me.
You're the biggest part of me.

Bless the Beasts and Children

Words and Music by Barry DeVorzon and Perry Botkin, Jr.

from the film *Bless the Beasts and Children*
recorded by The Carpenters

Bless the beasts and the children,
For in this world they have no voice,
They have no choice.
Bless the beasts and the children,
For the world can never be,
The world they see.

Refrain:
Light their way
When the darkness surrounds them;
Give them love, let it shine all around them.
Bless the beasts and the children;
Give them shelter from a storm;
Keep them safe;
Keep them warm.

Refrain

Bless the beasts and the children;
Give them shelter from a storm;
Keep them safe;
Keep them warm.

Breathe

Words and Music by Holly Lamar and Stephanie Bentley

recorded by Faith Hill

I can feel the magic floating in the air.
Being with you gets me that way.
I watch the sunlight dance across your face
And I never been this swept away.

All my thoughts just seem to settle on
    the breeze,
When I'm lyin' wrapped up in your arms.
The whole world just fades away,
The only thing I hear is the beating of
    your heart.

Refrain:
'Cause I can feel you breathe,
It's washing over me,
And suddenly I'm melting into you.
There's nothing left to prove,
Baby, all we need is just to be
Caught up in the touch,
The slow and steady rush.
Baby, isn't that the way
That love's supposed to be?
I can feel you breathe.
Just breathe.

In a way I know my heart is wakin' up
As all the walls come tumbling down.
Closer than I've ever felt before,
And I know and you know
There's no need for words right now.

Refrain

Caught up in the touch,
The slow and steady rush.
Baby, isn't that the way
That love's supposed to be?
I can feel you breathe.
Just breathe.
I can feel the magic floating in the air.
Bein' with you gets me that way.

Carolina in My Mind

Words and Music by James Taylor

recorded by James Taylor

Refrain:
In my mind I'm gone to Carolina.
Can't you see the sunshine?
And can't you just feel the moonshine?
And ain't it just like a friend of mine to
   hit me from behind?
And I'm gone to Carolina in my mind.

Karin she's a silver sun,
You'd best walk her away and watch
   it shine.
Watch her watch the morning come.
A silver tear appearing
Now I'm crying, ain't I?
I'm gone to Carolina in my mind.

There ain't no doubt in no one's mind
That love's the finest thing around.
Whisper something soft and kind.
And hey, babe, the sky's on fire,
I'm dying, ain't I?
I'm gone to Carolina in my mind.

Refrain

Dark and silent late last night,
I think I might have heard the highway call.
Geese in flight and dogs that bite.
And signs that might be omens say I'm going,
   going.
I'm gone to Carolina in my mind.

Now with a holy host of others standing
   'round me no,
Still I'm on the dark side of the moon.
And it seems like it goes on like this forever,
You must forgive me.
If it's up in...

Refrain Twice

Can't We Try

Words and Music by Dan Hill
Additional Lyrics by Beverly Chapin-Hill

recorded by Dan Hill & Vonda Sheppard

He:
I see your face cloud over like a little girl's
And your eyes have lost their shine.
You whisper something softly I'm not
    meant to hear.
Baby, tell me what's on your mind.

She:
I don't care what people say
About the two of us from diff'rent worlds.
I love you so much that it hurts inside.
Are you listening?

He:
Please listen to me, girl.

Refrain (Both):
Can't we try just a little bit harder?
Can't we give just a little bit more?
Can't we try to understand
That it's love we're fightin' for?
Can't we try just a little more passion?
Can't we try just a little less pride?
Love you so much, baby,
That it tears me up inside.

He:
I hear you on the telephone with God
    knows who,
Spilling out your heart for free.
Ev'ryone has someone they can talk to.
Girl, that someone should be me.

She:
So many times I've tried to tell you.
You just turned away.

He:
How did I know?

She:
My life is changing so fast now,
Leaves me lonely and afraid.

He:
Don't be afraid, no.

Refrain (Both)

He:
Don't let our love fade away.

She:
Don't let our love fade away.

He:
No matter what people say.

She:
No matter, no matter what they say.

He:
I need you more and more each day.

She:
Don't let our love fade away.

He:
No matter what people say.

She:
No matter, no matter what they say.

He:
Can't we try just a little bit harder?

She:
Can't we give just a little bit more?

Refrain (Both)

Can't we give a little bit, little bit?
Just a little bit harder?
Can't we give? Oh, can't we try?

Change the World

Words and Music by Wayne Kirkpatrick, Gordon Kennedy and Tommy Sims

featured on the Motion Picture Soundtrack *Phenomenon*
recorded by Wynonna, Eric Clapton

If I can reach the stars, pull one down for you,
Shine it on my heart so you could see the truth.
Then this love I have inside is everything it seems,
But for now I find it's only in my dreams
That I can change the world.
I will be the sunlight in your universe.

You would think my love was really something good,
Baby, if I could
Change the world.

If I could be king, even for a day,
I'd take you as my queen, I'd have it no other way.
And our love will rule in this kingdom we have made.
'Til then I'd be a fool wishing for the day
That I could change the world.

I would be the sunlight in your universe.
You would think my love was really something good,
Baby, if I could
Change the world.

Baby, if I could
Change the world.

I could change the world.
I would be the sunlight in your universe.
You would think my love was really something good,
Baby, if I could,
Change the world,
Baby, if I could
Change the world,
Baby if I could
Change the world.

Child of Mine

Words and Music by Carole King and Gerry Goffin

recorded by Carole King

Although you see the world
Different from me,
Sometimes I can touch upon
The wonders that you see.
All the new colors
And pictures you've designed.

Refrain:
Oh, yes sweet darling,
So glad you are a child of mine,
Child of mine,
Child of mine,
Oh, yes sweet darling,
So glad you are a child of mine.

You don't need directions,
You know which way to go
And I don't want to hold you back,
I just want to watch you grow.
You're the one who taught me
You don't have to look behind.

Refrain

Nobody's gonna kill your dreams
Or tell you how to live your life.
There'll always be people to make it hard for
    a while
But you'll change their heads when they see
    you smile.

The times you were born in
May not have been the best,
But you can make the times to come
Better than the rest,
I know you will be honest
If you can't always be kind,

Refrain Twice

Circle of Life

Music by Elton John
Lyrics by Tim Rice

from Walt Disney Pictures' *The Lion King*
recorded by Elton John

From the day we arrive on the planet
And blinking, step into the sun,
There's more to be seen than can
   ever be seen,
More to do than can ever be done.

Some say, "Eat or be eaten."
Some say, "Live and let live."
But all are agreed
As they join the stampede,
You should never take more than you give
In the circle of life.

It's the wheel of fortune.
It's the leap of faith.
It's the band of hope
'Til we find our place
On the path unwinding
In the circle of life.

Some of us fall by the wayside,
And some of us soar to the stars.
And some of us sail through our troubles,
And some have to live with the scars.
There's far too much to take in here,
More to find than can ever be found.
But the sun rolling high
Through the sapphire sky
Keeps great and small on the endless round
In the circle of life.

Refrain Twice

On the path unwinding
In the circle,
The circle of life.

The Closer I Get to You

Words and Music by James Mtume and Reggie Lucas

recorded by Roberta Flack & Donny Hathaway

The closer I get to you,
The more you make me see;
By giving me all you've got,
Your love has captured me.
Over and over again,
I try to tell myself that we could never be more than friends;
And all the while inside I knew it was real,
The way you make me feel.

Repeat Song and Fade

Colors of the Wind

Music by Alan Menken
Lyrics by Stephen Schwartz

from Walt Disney's *Pocahontas*
performed by Vanessa Williams

You think you own whatever land
  you land on,
The earth is just a dead thing you can claim;
But I know every rock and tree and creature
Has a life, has a spirit, has a name.

You think the only people who are people
Are the people who look and think like you,
But if you walk in the footsteps of a stranger
You'll learn things you never knew
  you never knew.

Have you ever heard the wolf cry to the
  blue corn moon
Or asked the grinning bobcat why
  he grinned?
Can you sing with all the voices of
  the mountain?
Can you paint with all the colors
  of the wind?
Can you paint with all the colors
  of the wind?

Come run the hidden pine trails
  of the forest,
Come taste the sun-sweet berries
  of the earth,
Come roll in all the riches all around you,
And for once never wonder what
  they're worth.

The rainstorm and the river are my brothers,
The heron and the otter are my friends,
And we are all connected to each other,
In a circle in a hoop that never ends.

Have you ever heard the wolf cry to the
  blue corn moon
Or let the eagle tell you where he's been?
Can you sing with all the voices of
  the mountain?
Can you paint with all the colors of the wind?
Can you paint with all the colors of the wind?

How high does the sycamore grow?
If you cut it down then you'll never know.

And you'll never hear the wolf cry to the blue
  corn moon.
For whether we are white or copper–skinned,
We need to sing with all voices
  of the mountain,
We need to paint with all the colors
  of the wind.
You can own the earth and still all you'll own
  is earth until
You can paint with all the colors of the wind.

Come In from the Rain

Words and Music by Melissa Manchester and Carole Bayer Sager

recorded by Captain & Tennille

Well, hello there,
Good old friend of mine,
You've been reaching for yourself
For such a long time.
There's so much to say,
No need to explain,
Just an open door for you
To come in from the rain.

It's a long road
When you're on your own,
And a man like you
Will always choose
The long way home.
There's no right or wrong,
I'm not here to blame.
I just want to be the one
To keep you from the rain,
From the rain.

Refrain:
And it looks like sunny skies
Now that I know you're all right.
Time has left us older and wiser,
I know I am.

And it's good to know
My best friend has come home again.
And I think of us like an old cliché.
But it doesn't matter
'Cause I love you, anyway;
Come in from the rain.

Refrain

And it's good to know
My best friend has come home again.
'Cause I think of us like an old cliché.
But it doesn't matter
'Cause I love you, anyway;
Come in from the rain.
Come in from the rain.
Come in from the rain.

Come to My Window

Words and Music by Melissa Etheridge

recorded by Melissa Etheridge

Refrain:
Come to my window.
Crawl inside, wait by the light of the moon.
Come to my window.
I'll be home soon.

I would dial the numbers
Just to listen to your breath.
And I would stand inside my hell
And hold the hand of death.
You don't know how far I'd go
To ease this precious ache.
And you don't know how much I'd give
Or how much I can take.
Just to reach you.
Just to reach you.
Oh, to reach you, oh.

Refrain

Keeping my eyes open,
I cannot afford to sleep.
Giving away promises
I know that I can't keep.
Nothing fills the blackness
That has seeped into my chest.
I need you in my blood,
I am forsaking all the rest.
Just to reach you.
Just to reach you.
Oh, to reach you, oh.

Refrain

I don't care what they think.
I don't care what they say.
What do they know about this love anyway?

Come, come to my window,
I'll be home, I'll be home, I'll be home.
I'm coming home.

Refrain

I'll be home, I'll be home, I'm comin' home.

Could It Be Magic

Words and Music by Barry Manilow and Adrienne Anderson

recorded by Barry Manilow

Spirit move me, every time I'm near you,
Whirling like a cyclone in my mind.
Sweet Melissa, angel of my lifetime,
Answer to all answers I can find;
Baby I love you.

Refrain:
Come, come, come into my arms.
Let me know the wonder of all of you.
Baby, I want you.
Now, now, now and hold on fast.
Could this be the magic at last?
Lady take me high upon a hillside,
High up where the stallion meets the sun.
I could love you; building my world around you,
Never leave you till my life is done;
Baby, I love you.

Refrain

Could it be magic?
Come, come, come into my arms.
Let me know the wonder of all of you.

The Crying Game

Words and Music by Geoff Stephens

featured in the film *The Crying Game*
recorded by Brenda Lee, Boy George

Refrain:
I know all there is to know about the crying game.
I've had my share of the crying game.
First, there are kisses, then there are sighs,
And then before you know where you are,
You're saying goodbye.

One day soon,
I'm gonna tell the moon about the crying game.
And if he knows maybe he'll explain,
Why there are heartaches,
Why there are tears,
And how to stop feeling blue
When love disappears.

Refrain

Don't want no more of the crying game.
I don't want no more if the crying game.
Oh!

Déjà Vu

Lyrics by Adrienne Anderson
Music by Isaac Hayes

recorded by Dionne Warwick

This is insane;
All you did was say hello, speak my name.
Feeling your love, like a love I used to know, long ago.
How can it be?
You're a different space and time, come to me.
Feeling I'm home, in a place I used to know, long ago.

Refrain:
Déjà vu,
Could you be the dream that I once knew?
Is it you?
Déjà vu,
Could you be the dream that might come true?
Shining through?

This is divine;
I've been waiting all my life, filling time.
Looking for you, nights were more than you could know, long ago.

Come to me now;
We don't have to dream of love, we know how.
Somewhere before it's as if I love you so long ago.

Refrain

I keep remembering me, I keep remembering you,
Déjà vu.

Repeat Refrain and Fade

Diary

Words and Music by David Gates

recorded by Bread

I found her diary underneath the tree
And started reading about me.
The words she'd written took me by
   surprise.
You'd never read them in her eyes.
They said that she had found the love
   she's waited for.
Wouldn't you know it.
She wouldn't show it.

Then she confronted with the
   writing there,
Simply pretending not to care.
I passed it off as just in keeping with
Her total disconcerting air.
And though she tried to hide
The love that she denied.
Wouldn't you know it,
She wouldn't show it.

And as I go through my life
I will give to her my wife,
All the sweet things I can find.

I found her diary underneath a tree
And started reading about me.
The words began to stick, then tears to fall.
Her meaning now was clear to see.
The love she's waited for
Was someone else, not me.
Wouldn't you know it,
She wouldn't show it.

And as I go through my life
I will wish for her, his wife,
All the sweet things she can find,
All the sweet things she can find.

(I Just) Died in Your Arms

Words and Music by Nicholas Eede

recorded by Cutting Crew

I keep looking for something I can't get.
Broken hearts lie all around me,
And I don't see an easy way to get out of this.
Her diary, it sits on the bedside table.
The curtains are closed, the cat's in the cradle.
Who would have thought that a boy like me could come to this.

Refrain:
Oh, I, I just died in your arms tonight.
It must've been something you said;
I just died in your arms tonight.
Oh, 'cause I just died in your arms tonight.
It must've been some kind of kiss;
I should've walked away,
I should've walked away.

Is there any just cause for feeling like this?
On the surface I'm a name on a list.
I try to be discreet, but then blow it again.
I've lost and found, it's my final mistake,
She's loving by proxy, no give and all take.
'Cause I've been thrilled to fantasy one too many times

Refrain

It was a long hot night.
She made it easy, she made it feel right.
But now it's over, the moment has gone.
I followed my hands, not my head; I know I was wrong.

Refrain

Do You Know Where You're Going To?

Words by Gerry Goffin
Music by Mike Masser

Theme from the film *Mahogany*
recorded by Diana Ross

Refrain:
Do you know
Where you're going to?
Do you like the things that life is showing you?
Where are you going to?
Do you know?

Do you get
What you're hoping for?
When you look behind you there's no open door.
What are you hoping for,
Do you know?

Once we were standing still in time,
Chasing the fantasies that filled our minds.
And you knew
How I loved you but my spirit was free,
Laughing at the questions that you once asked of me.

Refrain

No looking back at all we planned,
We let so many dreams just slip through our hands.
Why must we wait so long before we see
How sad the answers to those questions can be?

Refrain

Don't Cry Out Loud

Words and Music by Carole Bayer Sager and Peter Allen

recorded by Melissa Manchester

Baby cried the day the circus came to town,
'Cause she didn't like parades just passing by her.
So she painted on a smile and took up with some clown,
And she danced without a net up on the wire.
I know a lot about it 'cause you see,
Baby is an awful lot like me.

Refrain:
We don't cry out loud,
We just keep it inside,
Learn how to hide out feelings.
Fly high and proud.
And if you should fall,
Remember you almost had it all.

Baby cried the day they pulled the big top down,
They left behind her dreams among the litter.
And the different kind of love she thought she found,
Was nothing more than sawdust and some glitter.
But baby can't be broken 'cause you see,
She had the finest teacher, that's me.

I taught her don't cry out loud,
Just keep it inside,
Learn how to hide your feelings.
Fly high and proud.
And if you should fall,
Remember you almost had it all.

Refrain

Don't Fall in Love with a Dreamer

Words and Music by Kim Carnes and Dave Ellingson

recorded by Kenny Rogers with Kim Carnes

Just look at you sittin' there,
You never looked better than tonight.
And it'd be so easy to tell you I'd stay,
Like I've done so many times.

I was so sure this would be the night,
You'd close the door and wanna
   stay with me.
And it's be so easy to tell you I'd stay,
Like I've done so many times.

Don't fall in love with a dreamer,
'Cause he'll always take you in;
Just when you think you've really
   changed him,
He'll leave you again.

Don't fall in love with a dreamer,
'Cause he'll break you every time;
So, put out the light and just hold on,
Before we say goodbye.

Now it's morning and the phone rings,
And ya say you've gotta get your things
   together.
You just gotta leave before you change
   your mind.
And if you knew what I was thinkin', girl,
I'd turn around, if you'd ask me one
   more time.

Don't fall in love with a dreamer,
'Cause he'll always take you in.
Just when you think you've really
   changed him,
He'll leave you again.

Don't fall in love with a dreamer,
'Cause he'll break you every time;
So put out the light and just hold on,
Before we say goodbye,
Before we say goodbye, goodbye.

Don't Let Me Be Lonely Tonight

Words and Music by James Taylor

recorded by James Taylor

Do me wrong, do me right.
Tell me lies but hold me tight.
Save your goodbyes for the mornin' light,
But don't let me be lonely tonight.

Say goodbye and say hello.
Sure 'nuf good to see you but it's time to go.
Don't say yes, but please don't say no,
I don't want to be lonely tonight.

Go away then damn ya,
Go on and do as you please, yeah,
You ain't gonna see me gettin' down on my knees.
I'm undecided and your heart's been divided,
You've been turnin' my world upside down.

Do me wrong, do me right, right now, baby.
Go on and tell me lies but hold me tight.
Save your goodbyes for the mornin' light,
But don't let me be lonely tonight.
I don't want to be lonely tonight no, no
I don't want to be lonely tonight.

Easy

Words and Music by Lionel Richie

recorded by The Commodores

Know it sounds funny, but I just can't stand the pain;
Girl, I'm leaving you tomorrow.
Seems to me, girl, you know I've done all I can.
You see, I begged, stole, and I borrowed, yeah.

Refrain:
Ooh, that's why I'm easy.
I'm easy like Sunday morning.
That's why I'm easy.
I'm easy like Sunday morning.

Why in the world would anybody put chains on me?
I've paid my dues to make it.
Everybody wants me to be what they want me to be.
I'm not happy when I try to fake it, no.

Refrain

I wanna be high, so high.
I wanna be free to know the things I do are right.
I wanna be free, just me, oh, babe.

Repeat and Fade:
That's why I'm easy.
I'm easy like Sunday morning.
That's why I'm easy.
I'm easy like Sunday morning.

Ebony and Ivory

Words and Music by McCartney

recorded by Paul McCartney & Stevie Wonder

Refrain:
Ebony and ivory
Live together in perfect harmony,
Side by side on my piano keyboard,
Oh Lord, why don't we?

We all know that people are the same wherever you go.
There is good and bad in everyone,
We learn to live,
We learn to give each other what we need to survive,
Together alive.

Refrain

Ebony and ivory
Living together in perfect harmony.

End of the Road

Words and Music by Babyface, L.A. Reid and Daryl Simmons

from the Paramount Motion Picture *Boomerang*
recorded by Boyz II Men

Spoken:
Girl, you know we belong together.
I don't have no time for you to be playin'
    with my heart like this.
You'll be mine forever, baby, you just see.

Sung:
We belong together
And you know that I'm right.
Why do you play with my heart?
Why do you play with my mind?
You said we'd be forever,
Said it's never die.

How could you love and leave me
    and never say goodbye?
Well, I can't sleep at night without
    holding you tight.
Girl, each time I try I just break down
    and cry.
Pain in my head, oh, I'd rather be dead,
Spinnin' around and around.

Refrain:
Although we've come
To the end of the road,
Still I can't let you go.
It's unnatural.
You belong to me,
I belong to you.
Come to the end of the road,
Still I can't let you go.
It's unnatural.
You belong to me,
I belong to you, oh.

Girl, I know you really love me,
You just don't realize.
You've never been there before,
It's only your first time.
Maybe I'll forgive you,
Maybe you'll try.
We should be happy together forever,
    you and I.
Could you love me again like you loved
    me before?
This time I want you to love me much more.
This time instead, just come to my bed
And, baby, just don't let me down.

Refrain Twice

Spoken:
Girl, I'm here for you.
All those times at night when you
      just hurt me,
And just ran out with that other fellow,
Baby, I knew about it.
I just don't understand how much
      I love you, do you?
I'm here for you.
I'm not out to go out there
And cheat all night just like you did, baby.
But that's alright, huh, I love you anyway.
And I'm still gonna be here for you
'Til my dyin' day baby.
Right now, I'm just in so much pain, baby.
'Cause you just won't come back to me,
      will you?
Just come back to me.

Yes, baby, my heart is lonely.
My heart hurts, baby, yes, I feel pain too.
Baby please...

Even Now

Lyric by Marty Panzer
Music by Barry Manilow

recorded by Barry Manilow

Even now when there's someone else who cares,
When there's someone home who's waiting just for me.
Even now I think about you as I'm climbing up the stairs,
And I wonder what to do so she won't see...

That even now I know it wasn't right,
And I've found a better life than what we had.
Even now I wake up crying in the middle of the night,
And I can't believe it still could hurt so bad.

Even now when I have come so far,
I wonder where you are,
I wonder why it's still so hard without you,
Even now when I come shining through,
I swear I think of you, and how much I wish you knew
Even now.

Even now when I never hear your name,
And the world has changed so much since you've been gone.
Even now I still remember and the feeling's still the same,
And the pain inside of me goes on and on.
Even now.

Repeat Verse 3

Every Woman in the World

Words and Music by Dominic Bugatti and Frank Musker

recorded by Air Supply

Overnight scenes, dinner and wine,
Saturday girls.
I was never in love, never had the time
In my hustle and hurry world.
I was laughing myself to sleep, waking up lonely.
I needed someone to hold me.

It's such a crazy old town, it can drag you down
Till you run out of dreams.
So you party all night to the music and lights,
But you don't know what happy means.
I was dancing in the dark with strangers, no love around me,
When suddenly you found me.

Refrain:
Oh, girl you're ev'ry woman in the world to me.
You're my fantasy, you're my reality.
Girl, you're ev'ry woman in the world to me.
You're ev'rything I need, you're ev'rything to me, oh girl.

Ev'rything good, ev'rything fine,
That's what you are.
So put your hand in mine and together we'll climb
As high as the highest star.
I'm living a lifetime in ev'ry minute that we're together.
And I'm staying right here forever.

Refrain

I'll never let you go, never let you go.
Ev'ry woman in the world,
You're my fantasy, you're my fantasy.
Ev'ry woman in the world,
Ev'rything I need, ev'rything to me.

Everytime You Go Away

Words and Music by Daryl Hall

recorded by Paul Young

Hey, if we can't solve any problems,
Then why do we lose so many tears?
Oh, so you go again, when the leading man appears.
Always the same theme;
Can't you see we've got everything
Going on and on and on.

Refrain:
Every time you go away,
You take a piece of me with you.
Every time you go away,
You take a piece of me with you.

Go on and go free,
Maybe you're too close to see.
I can feel your body move,
Doesn't mean that much to me.
I can't go on singing the same theme;
'Cause can't you see we've got everything, baby,
Even though you know,

Refrain

I can't go on singing the same theme,
'Cause baby, can't you see
We got everything going on and on and on.

Refrain

Feel Like Makin' Love

Words and Music by Eugene McDaniels

recorded by Roberta Flack

Strollin' in the park,
Watchin' winter turn to spring.
Walkin' in the dark,
Seein' lovers do their thing.

Refrain:
That's the time
I feel like makin' love to you.
That's the time
I feel like makin' dreams come true.
Oh, baby.

When you talk to me,
When you're moanin' sweet and low.
When you're touchin' me
And my feelings start to show.

Refrain

In a restaurant,
Holdin' hands by candlelight.
While I'm touchin' you,
Wanting you with all my might.

Refrain

Repeat Verse 1 and Refrain

Feelings (¿Dime?)

English Words and Music by Morris Albert and Louis Gaste
Spanish Words by Thomas Fundora

recorded by Morris Albert

Feelings,
Nothing more than feelings,
Trying to forget my
Feelings of love.

Teardrops
Rolling down on my face,
Trying to forget my
Feelings of love.

Feelings,
For all my life I'll feel it.
I wish I'd never met you, girl;
You'll never come again.

Feelings,
Wo wo wo feelings.
Wo wo wo feel you
Again in my arms.

Feelings,
Feelings like I've never lost you,
And feelings like I'll never have you
Again in my heart.

Feelings,
For all my life I'll feel it.
I wish I'd never met you, girl;
You'll never come again.

Feelings,
Feelings like I've never lost you,
And feelings like I'll never have you
Again in my life.

Feelings,
Wo wo wo feelings,
Wo wo wo feelings,
Again in my arms.

Fire and Rain

Words and Music by James Taylor

recorded by James Taylor

Just yesterday morning they let me know
   you were gone,
Susan the plans they made put
   an end to you.
I walked out this morning and I wrote
   down this song,
I just can't remember who to send it to.

Refrain:
I've seen fire and I've seen rain.
I've seen sunny days that I thought would
   never end.
I've seen lonely times when I could not
   find a friend,
But I always thought that I'd see you again.

Won't you look down upon me Jesus,
You've got to help me make a stand.
You've just got to see me through
   another day.
My body's aching and my time is at hand,
And I won't make it any other way.

Refrain

Now I'm walking my mind to an easy time,
My back turned toward the sun.
Lord knows when the cold wind blows
It'll turn your head around.
There's hours of time on the telephone lines,
To talk about things to come.
Sweet dreams and flying machines in pieces
   on the ground.

Refrain

Thought I'd see you one more time again,
There's just a few things coming my way
   this time around,
Thought I'd see you,
Thought I'd see you one more time.
Fire and rain now…

Fly Away

Words and Music by John Denver

recorded by John Denver

All of her days have gone soft and cloudy.
All of her dreams have gone dry.
All of her nights have gone sad and shady,
She's getting ready to fly.

Refrain 1:
Fly away.
Fly away.
Fly away.

Life in the city can make you crazy
For sounds of the sand and the sea.
Life in a highrise can make you hungry
For things that can't even see.

Refrain 1

Refrain 2:
In this whole world
There's nobody as lonely as she.
There's nowhere to go,
And there's nowhere that she'd rather be.

She's looking for lovers and children playing,
She's looking for signs of the spring.
She listens for laughter and sounds of dancing,
She listens for any old thing.

Refrain 1

Refrain 2

Repeat Verse 1

From a Distance

Words and Music by Julie Gold

recorded by Bette Midler

From a distance the world looks blue
  and green,
And the snow-capped mountains white.
From a distance the ocean meets
  the stream
And the eagle takes to flight.

From a distance there is harmony,
And it echoes through the land.
It's the voice of hope, it's the voice
  of peace
It's the voice of every man.

Refrain:
God is watching us,
God is watching us,
God is watching us
From a distance.

From a distance we all have enough,
And no one is in need.
There are no guns, no bombs,
  no diseases,
No hungry mouths to feed.

From a distance we are instruments,
Marching in a common band.
Playing songs of hope, playing songs
  of peace,
They're the songs of every man.

Refrain

From a distance you look like my friend,
Even though we are at war.
From a distance I can't comprehend
What all this war is for.

From a distance there is harmony,
And it echoes through the land.
It's the voice of hopes, it's the love of loves,
It's the heart of every man.

It's the hope of hopes,
It's the love of loves,
It's the song of every man.

Georgia on My Mind

Words by Stuart Gorrell
Music by Hoagy Carmichael

a standard recorded by Ray Charles, Willie Nelson and various other artists

Georgia, Georgia, the whole day through,
Just an old sweet song keeps
Georgia on my mind.
(Georgia on my mind.)

Georgia, Georgia, a song of you,
Come as sweet and clear as moonlight through the pines.
Other arms reach out to me;
Other eyes smile tenderly;
Still in peaceful dreams I see
The road leads back to you,
Georgia, Georgia, no peace I find,
Just an old sweet song keeps
Georgia on my mind.

Glory of Love

Words and Music by David Foster, Peter Cetera and Diane Nini

Theme from *Karate Kid Part II*
recorded by Peter Cetera

Tonight it's very clear,
As we're both standing here,
There's so many things I want to say.
I will always love you,
I will never leave you alone.

Sometimes I just forget,
Say things I might regret,
It breaks my heart to see you crying.
I don't want to lose you,
I could never make it alone.

Refrain:
I am a man
Who would fight for your honor,
I'll be the hero you're dreaming of.
We'll live forever,
Knowing together,
That we did it all
For the glory of love.
You keep me standing tall,
You help me through it all,
I'm always strong
When you're beside me.
I have always needed you,
I could never make it alone.

Refrain

Just like the a knight in shining armor,
From a long time ago,
Just in time I will save the day,
Take you to my castle far away.

I am the man
Who will fight for your honor,
I'll be the hero that you're dreaming of.
We're gonna live forever,
Knowing together,
That we did it all
For the glory of love.

We'll live forever,
Knowing together,
That we did it all
For the glory of love.
We did it all for love.

Go the Distance

Music by Alan Menken
Lyrics by David Zippel

from Walt Disney Pictures' *Hercules*
recorded by Michael Bolton

I have often dreamed of a far-off place,
Where a hero's welcome
Would be waiting for me;
Where the crowds will cheer,
When they see my face,
And a voice keeps saying,
This is where I'm meant to be.
I'll be there someday.

I can go the distance.
I will find my way,
If I can be strong.
I know every mile
Will be worth my while.
When I go the distance,
I'll be right where I belong.

Down an unknown road,
To embrace my fate;
Though that road may wander,
It will lead me to you.
And a thousand years would be worth
   the wait.
It might take a lifetime,
But somehow I'll see it through.
And I won't look back.

I can go the distance.
And I'll stay on the track.
No, I won't accept defeat.
It's an uphill slope,
But I won't lose hope,
Till I go the distance,
And my journey is complete.
Oh, yeah.

But to look beyond the glory,
Is the hardest part,
For a hero's strength is measured,
By his heart.

Like a shooting star,
I will go the distance.
I will search the world.
I will face its harms.
I don't care how far.
I can go the distance,
Till I find my hero's welcome,
Waiting in your arms.

I will search the world.
I will face its harms,
Till I find my hero's welcome,
Waiting in your arms.

THE LYRIC LIBRARY

Goodbye to Love

Words and Music by Richard Carpenter and John Bettis

recorded by The Carpenters

I'll say goodbye to love.
No one ever cared if I should live or die.
Time and time again the chance for love has passed me by,
And all I know of love is how to live without it.
I just can't seem to find it.
So I've made my mind up I must live my life alone.
And though it's not the easy way,
I guess I've always known I'd say

Goodbye to love.
There are no tomorrows for this heart of mine.
Surely time will lose these bitter memories and I'll find,
That there is someone to believe in and to live for.
Something I could live for.
All the years of useless search have finally reached an end,
And loneliness and empty days will be my only friend.
From this day love is forgotten and I'll go on as best I can.

What lies in the future is a mystery to us all,
No one can predict the wheel of fortune as it falls,
There may come a time when I will see that I've been wrong.
But for now this is my song.
And it's goodbye to love,
I'll say goodbye to love.

Guilty

Words and Music by Barry Gibb, Maurice Gibb and Robin Gibb

recorded by Barbra Streisand & Barry Gibb

Shadows falling, baby,
We stand alone
Out on the street anybody you meet
Got a heartache of their own.
Make it a crime to be lonely or sad
You got a reason for living
You battle on
With the love you're livin' on you
    gotta be mine.
We take it away.
It's gotta be night and day
Just a matter of time.

Refrain:
And we got nothing to be guilty of
Our love will climb any mountain
Near or far, we are
And we never let it end.
We are devotion
And we got nothing to be sorry for
Our love is one in a million.
Eyes can see that we got a highway
    to the sky.
I don't want to hear your goodbye.

Pulse's racing, darling,
How grand we are.
Little by little we meet in the middle
There's danger in the dark.
Make it a crime to be out in the cold.
You got a reason for livin'
You battle on
With the love you're buildin' on you
    gotta be mine.
We take it away.
It's gotta be night and day
Just a matter of time.

Refrain

Don't wanna hear your goodbye.
I don't wanna hear your—
And we got nothing,

Refrain

Hands of Time

Words by Alan Bergman and Marilyn Bergman
Music by Michel Legrand

Theme from the Screen Gems Television Production *Brian's Song*

If the hands of time
Were hands that I could hold,
I'd keep them warm and in my hands
They'd not turn cold.

Hand in hand we'd choose
The moments that should last.
The lovely moments that
Should have no future and no past.

The summer from the top of the swing,
The comfort in the sound of a lullaby,
The innocence of leaves in the spring,
But most of all the moment
When love first touched me!

All the happy days
Would never learn to fly,
Until the hands of time
Would choose to wave "Goodbye."

Hard Habit to Break

Words and Music by Stephen Kipner and John Lewis Parker

recorded by Chicago

I guess I thought you'd be here forever,
Another illusion I chose to create.
You don't know what you got until it's gone,
And I found out a little too late.

I was acting as if
You were lucky to have me,
Doin' you a favor
(I hardly knew you were there.)
But then you were gone,
And it all was wrong,
Had no idea how much I cared.

Refrain:
Now being without you
Takes a lot of getting used to,
Should learn to live with it
But I don't want to.
Being without you
Is all a big mistake,
Instead of getting easier,
It's the hardest thing to take.
I'm addicted to you, babe,
You're a hard habit to break.

You found someone else, you had
    every reason,
You know I can't blame you for runnin'
    to him.
Two people together but livin' alone,
I was spreading my love too thin.

After all of these years
I'm still try'n to shake it,
Doin' much better.
(They say that it just takes time.)
But deep in the night,
It's an endless fight,
I can't get you out of my mind.

Refrain

Can't go on,
Just can't go on, on.
Can't go on,
Just can't go on, on.

Refrain

Hard to Say I'm Sorry

Words and Music by Peter Cetera and David Foster

recorded by Chicago

Everybody needs a little time away,
I heard her say,
From each other.
Even lovers need a holiday,
Far away
From each other.
Hold me now.
It's hard for me to say I'm sorry.
I just want you to stay.

After all that we've been through,
I will make it up to you.
I'll promise to.
And after all that's been said and done
You're just the part of me I can't let go.

Couldn't stand to be kept away,
Just for the day,
From your body.
Wouldn't wanna be swept away,
Far away,
From the one that I love.
Hold me now.
It's hard for me to say I'm sorry.
I just want you to know.
Hold me now.
I really want to tell you I'm sorry.
I could never let you go.

After all that we've been through,
I will make it up to you.
I'll promise to.
And after all that's been said and done
You're just the part of me I can't let go.
After all that we've been through,
I will make it up to you.
I'll promise to.
You're gonna be the lucky one.

Have You Ever Really Loved a Woman?

Words and Music by Bryan Adams, Michael Kamen and Robert John Lange

from the Motion Picture *Don Juan DeMarco*
recorded by Bryan Adams

To really love a woman
To understand her, you gotta know her deep inside;
Hear every thought, see every dream,
'N' give her wings when she wants to fly.
Then when you find yourself lyin' helpless in her arms,
Ya know ya really love a woman.

Refrain:
When you love a woman you tell her that she's really wanted.
When you love a woman you tell her that she's the one.
'Cause she needs somebody to tell her
That it's gonna last forever.
So tell me,
Have you ever really, really, really ever loved a woman?

To really love a woman,
Let her hold you 'til ya know how she needs to be touched.
You've gotta breathe her, really taste her,
'Til you can feel her in your blood.
'N' when you can see you unborn children in her eyes,
Ya know ya really love a woman.

Refrain

You got to give her some faith, hold her tight.
A little tenderness, gotta treat her right.
She will be there for you, takin' good care of you.
Ya gotta love your woman…

He Ain't Heavy...He's My Brother

Words and Music by Bob Russell and Bobby Scott

recorded by The Hollies, Neil Diamond

The road is long
With many a winding turn
That leads us to
Who knows where, who knows where.
But I'm strong
Strong enough to carry him.
He ain't heavy,
He's my brother.

So on we go.
His welfare is my concern.
No burden is he to bear.
We'll get there.
For I know
He would not encumber me.
He ain't heavy,
He's my brother.

If I'm laden at all,
I'm laden with sadness
That everyone's heart
Isn't filled with the gladness
Of love for one another.

It's a long, long road
From which there is no return.
While we're on our way to there,
Why not share?
And the load doesn't weigh
Me down at all.
He ain't heavy,
He's my brother.

Heaven in Your Eyes

Words and Music by Paul Dean, Mike Reno, John Dexter and Mae Moore

from the Paramount Motion Picture *Top Gun*
recorded by Loverboy

I can tell by the look in your eyes you've been hurting;
You know I'll never let you down, oh no.
And I'll try anything to keep it working.
You gave me time to find out what my heart was looking for
And what I'm feeling inside.

Refrain:
I want to see your love again in your eyes;
I never want this feeling to end.
It took some time to find the light,
But now I realize
I can see the heaven in your eyes.

Can't you see I'm finding it hard to let go?
All the heartaches we've been through.
I never really thought I'd see this love grow.
But you helped me to see;
I know what my heart's been looking for
And what I'm feeling inside.

Refrain

We've been living on the edge,
Where only the strong survive.
We've been living on the edge,
And it's something that we just can't hide.
Oh, this feeling inside.

Refrain

Oh, yeah, I can see the heaven in your eyes.
(Heaven in your eyes.)
I can see the heaven in your eyes.

Here You Come Again

Words by Cynthia Weil
Music by Barry Mann

recorded by Dolly Parton

Here you come again,
Just when I've begun to get myself together.
You waltz right in the door,
Just like you've done before,
And wrap my heart 'round your little finger.

Here you come again,
Just when I'm about to make it work without you.
You look into my eyes,
And lie those pretty lies,
And pretty soon I'm wond'rin' how I came to doubt you.

Refrain:
All you gotta do is smile that smile
And there go all my defenses.
Just leave it up to you and in a little while
You're messin' up my mind and fillin' up my senses.

Here you come again,
Lookin' better than a body has a right to,
And shakin' me up so that all I really know
Is here you come again,
And here I go.

Refrain

Here you come again,
Lookin' better than a body has a right to,
And shakin' me up so that all I really know
Is here you come again,
And here I go.
Here I go.

Hero

Words and Music by Mariah Carey and Walter Afanasieff

recorded by Mariah Carey

There's a hero
If you look inside your heart.
You don't have to be afraid
Of what you are.
There's an answer
If you reach into your soul
And the sorrow that you know
Will melt away.

Refrain:
And then a hero comes along
With the strength to carry on
And you cast your fears aside
And you know you can survive.
So, when you feel like hope is gone
Look inside you and be strong
And you'll finally see the truth
That a hero lies in you.

It's a long road
When you face the world alone.
No one reaches out a hand
For you to hold.
You can find love
If you search within yourself
And the emptiness you felt
Will disappear.

Refrain

Lord knows
Dreams are hard to follow,
Don't let anyone tear them away.
Hold on,
There will be tomorrow.
In time you'll find the way.

Refrain

Hero

Words and Music by Enrique Iglesias, Paul Barry and Mark Taylor

recorded by Enrique Iglesias

Spoken:
Let me be your hero.

Sung:
Would you dance if I asked you to dance?
Would you run and never look back?
Would you cry if you saw me crying?
Would you save my soul tonight?

Would you tremble if I touched your lips?
Would you laugh? Oh, please tell me this.
Now would you die for the one you love?
Hold me in your arms tonight.

Refrain:
I can be your hero, baby.
I can kiss away the pain.
I will stand by you forever.
You can take my breath away.

Would you swear that you'll
    always be mine?
Would you lie? Would you run and hide?
Am I in too deep? Have I lost my mind?
I don't care, you're here tonight.

Refrain

Oh, I just want to hold you.
I just want to hold you, oh yeah.
Am I in too deep? Have I lost my mind?
Well, I don't care, you're here tonight.

Refrain (Twice)

You can take my breath away.
I can be your hero.

Holding Back the Years

Words by Mick Hucknall
Music by Mick Hucknall and Neil Moss

recorded by Simply Red

Holding back the years,
Thinking of the fear I've had so long
When somebody hears,
Listen to the fear that's gone.
Strangled by the wishes of Pater,
Hoping for the arms of Mater,
Get to meet her sooner or later.
I'll keep holding on. I'll keep holding on.

Holding back the years,
Chance for me to escape from all I've known.
Holding back the tears,
'Cause nothing here has grown.
I've wasted all my tears,
Wasted all those years.
Nothing had the chance to be good,
Nothing ever could.

Refrain:
I'll keep holding on.

Well I've wasted all my tears,
Wasted all of those years.
And nothing had a chance to be good,
'Cause nothing ever could.

Honesty

Words and Music by Billy Joel

recorded by Billy Joel

If you search for tenderness,
It isn't hard to find.
You can have the love you need to live.
And if you look for truthfulness
You might as well be blind
It always seems to be so hard to give.

Refrain:
Honesty
Is such a lonely word.
Everyone is so untrue.
Honesty
Is hardly ever heard,
But mostly what I need from you.

I can always find someone
To say they sympathize
If I wear my heart out on my sleeve.
But I don't want some pretty face
To tell me pretty lies.
All I want is someone to believe.

Refrain

I can find a lover,
I can find a friend,
I can have security
Until the bitter end.
Anyone can comfort me
With promises again
I know
I know.

When I'm deep inside of me
Don't be too concerned
I won't ask for nothin' while I'm gone.
When I want sincerity,
Tell me, where else can I turn?
Cause you're the one that I depend upon.

Refrain

How Am I Supposed to Live Without You

Words and Music by Michael Bolton and Doug James

recorded by Michael Bolton

I could hardly believe it
When I heard the news today.
I had to come and get it straight from you.
They said you are leavin'
Someone's swept your heart away.
From the look upon your face
I see it's true.
So tell me all about it
Tell me 'bout the plans you makin',
Oh, tell me one thing more
Before I go.

Refrain:
Tell me how am I
Supposed to live without you,
Now that I've
Been lovin' you so long?
How am I
Supposed to live without you?
And how am I
Supposed to carry on
When all that I've
Been living for is gone?

I'm too proud for crying,
Didn't come here to break down.
It's just a dream of mine is comin' to an end.
And how can I blame you
When I built my world around
The hope that one day we'd be
So much more than friends?
I don't want to know the price
I'm gonna pay for dreamin'
Oh, even now
It's more than I can take.

Refrain

Now I don't wanna know the price
I'm gonna pay for dreamin'
Oh, now that your dream has come true.

Refrain

How Can We Be Lovers

Words and Music by Desmond Child, Michael Bolton and Diane Warren

recorded by Michael Bolton

Refrain:
How can we be lovers if we can't be friends?
How can we start over when the fightin' never ends, baby?
How can we make love if we can't make amends?
How can we be lovers if we can't be, can't be friends?

Look at us now. Look at us, baby.
Still tryin' to work it out.
Never get it right.
We must be fools. We must be crazy
Woh, woh, there's been communication.
Woh, woh, it's a no-win situation.

Refrain

We lie awake. Discord between us.
We're just not talkin'. We got so much to say.
Let's break these chains. Our love can free us.
Woh, woh, ain't it time we started tryin'?
Woh, woh, can I stop this love from dyin'?

Refrain

Baby, how can we be lovers?
Baby, chances are that we can make it.
We can work it out.

Refrain Twice

How Can You Mend a Broken Heart

Words and Music by Barry Gibb and Robin Gibb

recorded by The Bee Gees

I can think of younger days when living for my life
Was everything a man could want to do.
I could never see tomorrow,
I was never told about the sorrow.

Refrain:
And how can you mend a broken heart?
How can you stop the rain from falling down?
How can you stop the sun from shining?
What makes the world go 'round?
How can you mend this broken man?
How can a loser ever win?
Please help me mend my broken heart
And let me live again.

I can still feel the breeze that rustles through the trees
And misty memories of days gone by.
We could never see tomorrow;
No one said a word about the sorrow.

Refrain

How Much I Feel

Words and Music by David Pack

recorded by Ambrosia

I don't know how this whole business
  started
Of you thinkin' that I have been untrue.
But if you think that we'd be better parted,
It's gonna hurt me, but I'll break away
  from you.
Well, just give me the sign and I will
  be gone, yeah.

Refrain:
That's how much I feel, feel for you, baby.
How much I need, well I need your touch.
How much I live, I live for your loving.
That's how much, that's how much,
That's how much, that's how much.

I sleep alone, and late at night
  I'm dreamin'
Of the togetherness that seems to be
  leaving me.
I'd give it all and then I'd give some more
If you would only love me like you
  had before.
Well, take hold of my hand and all
  will be forgiven, yeah.

Refrain

So you try, try to stay in the middle.
And then you cry, well you cry just a little.
Then you both realize
Just how foolish you've been.
And you try to make amends
But you're better off as friends.
'Cause that's how much, that's how much,
That's how much, that's how much.

How's your life been goin' on?
I've got a wife now. Years we've been
  goin' strong.
There's just something that I've got to say:
Sometimes when we make love,
I still can see your face.
Ooh, just try to recall
When we were as one, yeah.

Refrain

How Sweet It Is (To Be Loved by You)

Words and Music by Edward Holland, Lamont Dozier and Brian Holland

recorded by Marvin Gaye, James Taylor

Refrain:
How sweet it is to be loved by you.
How sweet it is to be loved by you.

I needed the shelter of someone's arms,
There you were.
I needed someone to understand my ups and downs,
There you were.
With sweet love and devotion,
Deeply touching my emotion.
I want to stop and thank you, baby;
I want to stop and thank you, baby, yes I do.

Refrain

I close my eyes at night,
Wonderin' where would I be without you in my life.
Ev'rything I did was just a bore,
Ev'rywhere I went, seems I've been there before.
But you brighten up for me all of my days
With a love so sweet in so many ways.
I want to stop and thank you, baby;
I want to stop and thank you, baby, yes I do.

Refrain

You were better to me than I was to myself.
For me there's you and there ain't nobody else.
I want to stop and thank you, baby;
I want to stop and thank you, baby, yes I do.

Refrain

I Am Woman

Words by Helen Reddy
Music by Ray Burton

recorded by Helen Reddy

I am woman, hear me roar,
In numbers too big to ignore,
And I know too much to go back to pretend.
'Cause I've heard it all before,
And I've been down there on the floor,
No one's ever gonna keep me down again.

Refrain:
Oh, yes I am wise, but it's wisdom born of pain.
Yes, I paid the price, but look how much I gained.
If I have to I can do anything.
I am strong, I am invincible,
I am woman.

You can bend but never break me,
'Cause it only serves to make me,
More determined to achieve my final goal.
And I come back even stronger,
Not a novice any longer,
'Cause you've deepened the conviction in my soul.

Refrain

I am woman!
I am woman!

I Am Your Child

Lyric by Marty Panzer
Music by Barry Manilow

recorded by Barry Manilow

I am your child.
Wherever you go,
You take me, too.
Whatever I know,
I learn from you.
Whatever I do,
You taught me to do.
I am your child.
And I am your chance.
Whatever will come,
Will come from me.
Tomorrow is won
By winning me.
Whatever I am,
You taught me to be.
I am your hope,
I am your chance,
I am your child.

(Everything I Do) I Do It for You

Words and Music by Bryan Adams, Robert John Lange and Michael Kamen

from the Motion Picture *Robin Hood: Prince of Thieves*
recorded by Bryan Adams

Look into my eyes,
You will see what you mean to me.
Search your heart, search your soul,
And when you find me there,
You will search no more.
Don't tell me it's not worth trying for.
You can't tell me it's not worth dying for.
You know it's true,
Everything I do,
I do it for you.

Look into your heart,
You will find there's nothing there
  to hide.
So, take me as I am, take my life,
I would give it all, I would sacrifice.
Don't tell me it's not worth fighting for.
I can't help it, there's nothing I
  want more.
You know it's true,
Everything I do,
I do it for you.

There's no love like your love,
And no other could give more love.
There's no way, unless you're there,
All the time, all the way, yeah.

Oh, you can't tell me it's not worth trying for.
I can't help it, there's nothing I want more.
Yeah, I would fight for you,
I'd lie for you, walk the wire for you,
Yeah, I'd die for you.
You know it's true,
Everything I do,
Oh, oh, I do it for you.

I Don't Have the Heart

Words and Music by Allan Rich and Jud Friedman

recorded by James Ingram

Your face is beaming.
You say it's 'cause you're dreaming
Of how good it's going to be.
You say you've been around,
And now you've finally found
Ev'rything you've wanted and need in me.

Refrain:
I don't have the heart to hurt you.
It's the last thing I wanna do.
But I don't have the heart to love you,
Not the way you want me to.

Inside I'm dying
To see you crying.
How can I make you understand?
I care about you,
So much about you, baby.
I'm tryin' to say this as gently as I can, 'cause

Refrain

You're so trusting and open,
Hoping that love will start.
But I don't have the heart.
Oh, no, I don't have the heart.

Refrain

I don't have the heart.
Baby, I don't have the heart.
I don't have the heart.

I Hope You Dance

Words and Music by Tia Sillers and Mark D. Sanders

recorded by Lee Ann Womack with Sons of the Desert

I hope you never lose your sense of wonder,
You get your fill to eat, but always keep that hunger.
May you never take one single breath for granted.
God forbid love ever leave you empty handed.
I hope you still feel small when you stand beside the ocean.
Whenever one door closes, I hope one more opens.
Promise me that you'll give faith a fighting chance.
And when you get the choice to sit it out or dance,
I hope you dance. I hope you dance.

I hope you never fear those mountains in the distance,
Never settle for the path of least resistance.
Livin' might mean takin' chances if they're worth takin'.
Lovin' might be a mistake, but it's worth makin'.
Don't let some hell-bent heart leave you bitter.
When you come close to sellin' out, reconsider.
Give the heavens above more than just a passing glance.
And when you get the choice to sit it out or dance,
I hope you dance. I hope you dance.

(Time is a wheel in constant motion, always rolling us along.
Tell me, who wants to look back on their youth
And wonder where those years have gone?)

I hope you still feel small when you stand beside the ocean.
Whenever one door closes, I hope one more opens.
Promise me that you'll give faith a fighting chance.
And when you get the choice to sit it out or dance,
Dance. I hope you dance.

(Time is a wheel in constant motion, always rolling us along.
Tell me, who wants to look back on their youth
And wonder where those years have gone?)

I Just Fall in Love Again

Words and Music by Larry Herbstritt, Stephen H. Dorff, Gloria Sklerov and Harry Lloyd

recorded by Anne Murray, The Carpenters

Dreamin', I must be dreamin';
Or am I really lyin' here with you?
Baby, you take me in your arms,
And though I'm wide awake
I know my dream is comin' true.

Refrain:
And, oh, I just fall in love again;
Just one touch and then it happens ev'ry time.
And there I go, I just fall in love again,
And when I do, I can't help myself,
I fall in love with you.

Magic, it must be magic,
The way I hold you and the night just seems to fly.
Easy for you to take me to a star.
Heaven is that moment when I look into your eyes.

Refrain

Can't help myself, I fall in love with you.

I Like Dreamin'

Words and Music by Kenny Nolan

recorded by Kenny Nolan

Refrain:
I like dreamin', 'cause dreamin' can make you mine.
I like dreamin', closin' my eyes and feelin' fine.
When the lights go down, I'm holdin' you so tight,
Gotcha in my arms, and it's paradise 'til the mornin' light.

I see us on the shore beneath the bright sunshine.
We walked along Saint Thomas beach a million times.
Hand in hand, two barefoot lovers kissin' in the sand.
Side by side, the tide rolls in,
I'm touchin' you, you're touching me,
If only it could be.

Refrain

Through each dream, how our love has grown.
I see us with our children and our happy home.
Little smiles, so warm and tender, lookin' up at us.
Blessed by love, the world we share
Until I wake, I reach for you, and you're just not there.

Refrain

I Need You

Words and Music by Dennis Matkosky and Ty Lacy

featured in the Epic Mini-Series *Jesus*
recorded by LeAnn Rimes

I don't need a lot of things;
I can get by with nothing.
Of all the blessings life can bring,
I've always needed something.
But I've got all I want
When it comes to loving You.
You're my only reason,
You're my only truth.

Refrain:
I need You like water,
Like breath, like rain.
I need You like mercy
From heaven's gate.
There's a freedom in Your arms
That carries me through.
I need You.

You're the hope that moves me
To courage again, oh yeah.
You're the love that rescues me
When the cold winds rage.
And it's so amazing,
'Cause that's just how You are.
And I can't turn back now,
'Cause You've brought me too far.

Refrain Twice

Oh, yes I do.

I Never Knew Love

Words and Music by Will Robinson and Larry Boone

recorded by Doug Stone

I never knew the power of a song
Till I heard the music playin'
The day momma passed on.
Never knew what innocence was about
Till the first time I laid eyes on the face
Of a newborn child.

Refrain:
I never knew love;
No, I mean real love.
I never knew that kind of love
Till this moment with you.

I never understand the meaning of home
Till I pulled into that old dirt drive
After being gone too long.
I didn't know what serenity really was
Till I stopped one day to listen to
That ol' river gently run.

Refrain

I've known the hunger before tonight for
    other loves.
I felt the yearning, I felt the fire in their
    touch.
But this goes deeper than anything I've ever
    known;
Beyond my heart, clear down to my soul.

I never knew what beauty could behold
Till you looked at me
And I could see forever unfold.
Oh, you made me whole.

Refrain

Till I was loved by you.

I Want to Know What Love Is

Words and Music by Mick Jones

recorded by Foreigner

I've gotta take a little time,
A little time to think things over.
I better read between the lines
In case I need it when I'm older.

Now, this mountain I must climb
Feels like the world upon my shoulders.
Through the clouds I see love shine.
It keeps me warm as life grows colder.

Refrain:
In my life
There's been heartache and pain.
I don't know if I can face it again.
Can't stop now.
I've traveled so far
To change this lonely life.
I want to know what love is.
I want you to show me.
I want to feel what love is.
I know you can show me.

I've gotta take a little time,
A little time to think things over.
I better read between the lines
In case I need it when I'm older.

I'm gonna take a little time,
A little time to look around me.
I've got nowhere left to hide.
It looks like love has finally found me.

Refrain

I want to know what love is.
I want you to show me.
I want to feel what love is.
I know you can show me.

I Will Remember You

Words and Music by Sarah McLachlan, Seamus Egan and Dave Merenda

Theme from the film *The Brothers McMullen*
recorded by Sarah McLachlan

Refrain:
I will remember you.
Will you remember me?
Don't let your life pass you by.
Weep not for the memories.

Remember the good times that we had.
We let them slip away from us when things got bad.
Clearly I first saw you smilin' in the sun.
Wanna feel your warmth upon me. I wanna be the one.

Refrain

I'm so tired but I can't sleep.
Standin' on the edge of something much too deep.
It's funny how I feel so much but I cannot say a word.
We are screaming inside or we can't be heard.

Refrain

I'm so afraid to love you, more afraid to lose,
Clinging to a past that doesn't let me choose.
Well once there was a darkness, a deep and endless night.
You gave me everything you had, oh, you gave me light.

Refrain Twice

Weep not for the memories.

I Won't Last a Day Without You

Words and Music by Paul Williams and Roger Nichols

recorded by The Carpenters

Day after day,
I must face a world of strangers where
  I don't belong.
I'm not that strong,
It's nice to know,
That there's someone I can turn to
  who will always care,
You're always there,

Refrain:
When there's no getting over that rainbow,
When my smallest of dreams won't
  come true,
I can take all the madness the world
  has to give,
But I won't last a day without you.

So many times,
When the city seems to be without a
  friendly face,
A lonely place,
It's nice to know,
That you'll be there if I need you and
  you'll always smile,
It's all worthwhile,

Refrain

Touch me and I end up singing,
Troubles seem to up and disappear,
You touch me with the love you're bringing,
I can't really lose when you're near.

When you're near my love,
If all my friends have forgotten half their
  promises
They're not unkind, just hard to find.
One look at you,
And I know that I could learn to live
  without the rest,
I found the best.

Refrain Twice

I Write the Songs

Words and Music by Bruce Johnston

recorded by Barry Manilow

I've been alive forever,
And I wrote the very first song.
I put the words and the melodies together,
I am music, and I write the songs.

Refrain:
I write the songs that make the whole world sing;
I write the songs of love and special things.
I write the songs that make the young girls cry;
I write the songs, I write the songs.

My home lies deep within you
And I've got my own place in your soul.
Now, when I look out through your eyes
I'm young again, even though I'm very old.

Refrain

Oh, my music makes you dance
And gives you a second chance,
And I wrote some rock 'n' roll
So you can move.

Music fills your heart,
Well, that's a real fine place to start.
It's from me, it's for you,
It's from you, it's for me
It's a world-wide symphony.

Refrain

I'd Rather Leave While I'm in Love

Words and Music by Carole Bayer Sager and Peter Allen

recorded by Rita Coolidge

I'd rather leave while I'm in love,
While I still believe the meaning of the word.
I keep my dreams and just pretend
That you and I were never meant to end.

Refrain:
Too many times I've seen the rose die on the vine.
And somebody's heart gets broken, usually it's mine.
I don't wanna take the chance of being hurt again,
And you and I can't say good-bye.

So, if you wake and find me gone,
Hey, babe, just carry on.
You see, I need my fantasy.
I still believe it's best to leave while I'm in love.

Refrain

So, if you wake and find me gone,
Hey, babe, just carry on.
You see, I need my fantasy.
I still believe it's best to leave while I'm in love.
I'd rather leave while I'm in love.

I'll Be Loving You (Forever)

Words and Music by Maurice Starr

recorded by New Kids On The Block

I'm not that kind of guy
Who can take a broken heart,
So don't ever leave.
I don't want to see us part.
The very thought
Of losing you
Means that ev'rything
Would go down under.

Refrain:
I'll be loving you forever,
Just as long as you want me to be.
I'll be loving you forever,
All this love's for you and me.
Yeah, I'll be loving you.
I'll be loving you.
The things you do.
I'll be loving you.
I'll be loving you.

I count the blessings
That keep our love new.
There's one for me
And a million for you.
There's just so much
That I want to say.
But when I look at you,
All my thoughts get in the way.

Refrain

We've learned to fall
To ev'ry turn by now.
This love will last forever.
I can see it all now.

I'll be loving you.
The things you,
I'll be loving you.

I'll Have to Say I Love You in a Song

Words and Music by Jim Croce

recorded by Jim Croce

Well, I know it's kind of late.
I hope I didn't wake you.
But what I got to say can't wait.
I know you'd understand.

Refrain:
'Cause ev'ry time I tried to tell you
The words just came out wrong.
So I'll have to say I love you in a song.

Yeah, I know it's kind of strange,
But ev'ry time I'm near you,
I just run out of things to say.
I know you'd understand.

Refrain

'Cause ev'ry time the time was right
All the words just came out wrong.
So I'll have to say I love you in a song.

Yeah, I know it's kind of late.
I hope I didn't wake you.
But there's something that I just got to say.
I know you'd understand.

Refrain

I'll Make Love to You

Words and Music by Babyface

recorded by Boyz II Men

Close your eyes, make a wish,
And blow out the candlelight
For tonight is just your night.
We're gonna celebrate
All through the night.

Pour the wine, light the fire.
Girl, your wish is my command.
I submit to your demands.
I will do anything.
Girl, you need only ask.

Refrain:
I'll make love to you
Like you want me to
And I'll hold you tight,
Baby, all through the night.
I'll make love to you
When you want me to
And I will not go
Till you tell me to.

Girl, relax,
Let's go slow.
I ain't got nowhere to go.
I'm just gonna concentrate on you.
Girl, are you ready?
It's gonna be a long night.

Throw your clothes
On the floor
I'm gonna take my clothes off too.
I made plans to be with you.
Girl, whatever you ask me,
You know I could do.

Refrain

Baby, tonight
Is your night
And I will do you right.
Just make a wish
On your night,
Anything that you ask.
I will give you the love of your life,
Your life, your life.

Refrain Twice

I'll Never Love This Way Again

Words and Music by Richard Kerr and Will Jennings

recorded by Dionne Warwick

You looked inside my fantasies and made each one come true,
Something no one else had ever found a way to do.
I've kept the memories one by one, since you took me in.

Refrain:
I know I'll never love this way again.
I know I'll never love this way again,
So I keep holdin' on before the good is gone.
I know I'll never love this way again,
Hold on, hold on, hold on.
A fool will lose tomorrow reaching back for yesterday.
I won't turn my head in sorrow if you should go away.
I'll stand here and remember just how good it's been.
And...

Refrain

I know I'll never love this way again,
So I keep holdin' on before the good is gone.
I know I'll never love this way again,
Hold on, hold on, hold on.

I'm Still in Love with You

Words and Music by Al Green, Willie Mitchell and Al Jackson, Jr.

recorded by Al Green

Spending my days thinking about you girl;
Being here with you, being here with you,
I can't explain myself, why I feel like I do,
'Tho it hurt me so to let you know.

And I look into your eyes,
And you let me know how you feel,
Let me know that love is really real.
And it seems to me,
That I'm wrapped up in your love.
Don't you know that I'm still in love,
Sho-nuff in love with you?
Well I know that I'm still in love,
Sho-nuff in love with you.

When I look into your eyes all the years.
How I see me loving you and you loving me.
It seems to me that I'm wrapped up in your love.
Don't you know that I'm still in love,
Sho-nuff in love with you?
I, I, don't you know that I'm still in love,
Sho-nuff in love with you?

If Ever You're in My Arms Again

Words and Music by Michael Masser, Tom Snow and Cynthia Weil

recorded by Peabo Bryson

It all came so easily, all the lovin'
   you gave me;
The feelings we shared.
And I can still remember how you
   touched me so tender.
It told me you care.

We had a once in a lifetime,
But I just couldn't see until it was gone.
A second once in a lifetime
May be too much to ask.
But I swear from now on;

Refrain:
If ever you're in my arms again,
This time I'll love you much better.
If ever you're in my arms again,
This time I'll hold you forever.
This time will never end.

Now I'm seein' clearly how I still need
   you near me;
The feelings we shared.
There's something between us that
   won't ever leave us.
There's no letting go.

We had a once in a lifetime,
But I just didn't know it till my
   life fell apart.
A second once in a lifetime
Isn't too much to ask.
'Cause I swear from now on;

Refrain

Never end.

The best of romancin' deserves
   second chances.
I'll get to you somehow.
'Cause I promise now;

Refrain

If I Could

Lyrics by Ron Miller
Music by Kenny Hirsch and Marti Sharron

recorded by Regina Belle, Barbra Streisand

If I could,
I'd protect you from the sadness in
    your eyes,
Give you courage in a world of
    compromise.
Yes, I would.
If I could,
I would teach you all the things
    I never learned.
And I'd help you cross the bridges
    that I burned.
Yes, I would.

If I could,
I would try to shield your innocence
    from time,
But the part of life I gave you isn't mine.
I watched you grow
So I could let you go.

If I could,
I would help you make it through the
    hungry years,
But I know that I can never cry your tears.
But I would
If I could.

If I live
In a time and place
Where you don't want to be,
You don't have to walk along this road
    with me.
My yesterday
Won't have to be your way.

If I knew,
I'd have tried to change the world I
    brought you to,
Through there wasn't very much that
    I could do.
But I still would
If I could.

If, if I could,
I would try to shield your innocence
    from time,
But the part of life I gave you isn't mine.
I watched you grow
So I could let you go.

If I could,
I would help you make it through the
    hungry years,
But I know that I can never cry your tears.
But I would
If I could.

Yes, I would.
Yes, I would
If I could.

If I Ever Lose My Faith in You

Written and Composed by Sting

recorded by Sting

You could say I lost my faith in science and progress.
You could say I lost my belief in the holy church.
You could say I lost my sense of direction.
You could say all of this and worse, but:

Refrain:
If I ever lose my faith in you
There'd be nothing left for me to do.

Some would say I was a lost man in a lost world.
You could say I lost my faith in the people on TV
You could say I lost my belief in our politicians.
They all seem like game show hosts to me.

Refrain

Hey, hey.
I could be lost inside their lies without a trace.
But every time I close my eyes I see your face.
I never saw no miracle of science
That didn't go from a blessing to a curse.
I never saw no military solution
That didn't always end up as something worse,
But, let me say this first:

If I ever lose my faith in you
If I ever lose my faith in you
There'd be nothing left for me to do.
There'd be nothing left for me to do.
If I ever lose my faith,
If I ever lose my faith,
If I ever lose my faith,
If I ever lose my faith in you...

If You Leave Me Now

Words and Music by Peter Cetera

recorded by Chicago

If you leave me now,
You'll take away the biggest part of me.
Ooh, no, baby please don't go.
And if you leave me now,
You'll take away the very heart of me.
Ooh girl, I just want you to stay.

A love like ours is love that's hard to find.
How could we let it slip away?
We've come too far to leave it all behind.
How could we end it all this way?

When tomorrow comes,
Then we'll both regret the things we said today.

If you leave me now,
You'll take away the biggest part of me.
Ooh, no, baby please don't go.

Repeat Song

Repeat and Fade:
Ooh, girl, I just want to have you by my side.
Ooh, no, baby please don't go.

Imagine

Words and Music by John Lennon

recorded by John Lennon

Imagine there's no heaven.
It's easy if you try.
No hell below us,
Above us only sky.
Imagine all the people
Living for today.

Imagine there's no countries.
It isn't hard to do.
Nothing to kill or die for
And no religion, too.
Imagine all the people
Living life in peace.

You may say I'm a dreamer.
But I'm not the only one.
I hope someday you'll join us
And the world will be as one.

Imagine no possessions.
I wonder if you can.
No need for greed or hunger,
A brotherhood of man.
Imagine all the people
Sharing all the world.

You may say I'm a dreamer.
But I'm not the only one.
I hope someday you'll join us
And the world will live as one.

In the Air Tonight

Words and Music by Phil Collins

recorded by Phil Collins

I can feel it coming
In the air tonight, oh Lord.
And I've been waiting for this moment
For all my life, oh Lord.
Can you feel it coming
In the air tonight, oh Lord, oh Lord.

Well, if you told me you were drowning,
I would not lend a hand.
I've seen your face before, my friend,
But I don't know if you know who I am.
Well, I was there and I saw what you did,
I saw it with my own two eyes.
So you can wipe off the grin,
I know where you've been,
It's all been a pack of lies.

Refrain:
And I can feel it coming
In the air tonight, oh Lord.
Well, I've been waiting for this moment
For all my life, oh Lord.
I can feel it coming
In the air tonight, oh Lord, oh Lord.

Well, I remember, I remember,
Don't worry, how could I ever forget.
It's the first time, the last time we ever met.
But I know the reason why you keep the
    silence up.
No, you don't fool me.
The hurt doesn't show,
But the pain still grows,
It's no stranger to you or me.

Refrain

I can feel it in the air tonight, oh Lord,
    oh Lord.
Well, I've been waiting for this moment
For all my life, oh Lord.
And I can feel it coming
In the air tonight, oh Lord.
Well, I've been waiting for this moment
For all my life, oh Lord.

Invisible Touch

Words and Music by Tony Banks, Phil Collins and Mike Rutherford

recorded by Genesis

Well, I've been waiting, waiting here so long,
But thinking nothing, nothing could go wrong.
But now I know she has a built-in ability
To take ev'rything she sees.
And now it seems I'm falling, falling for her.

Refrain:
She seems to have an invisible touch, yeah.
She reaches in and grabs right hold of your heart.
She seems to have an invisible touch, yeah.
It takes control and slowly tears you apart.

I don't really know her; I only know her name.
But she crawls under your skin, you're never quite the same.
And now I know she's got something you just can't trust,
Something mysterious.
And now it seems I'm falling, falling for her.

Refrain

She don't like losing; to her it's still a game.
And though she will mess up your life, you'll want her just the same,
And now I know she has a built-in ability
To take ev'rything she sees.
And now it seems I've fallen, fallen for her.

Refrain

Iris

Words and Music by John Rzeznik

from the Motion Picture *City of Angels*
recorded by Goo Goo Dolls

And I'd give up forever to touch you
'Cause I know that you feel me somehow.
You're the closest to heaven that I'll ever be
And I don't wanna go home right now.

And all I could taste is this moment,
And all I can breathe is your life.
And sooner or later it's over.
I just don't wanna miss you tonight.

Refrain:
And I don't want the world to see me
'Cause I don't think that they'd understand.
When everything's made to be broken
I just want you to know who I am.

And you can't fight the tears that ain't coming,
Or the moment of truth in your lies.
When everything feels like the movies,
Yeah, you bleed just to know you're alive.

Refrain Twice

Isn't She Lovely

Words and Music by Stevie Wonder

recorded by Stevie Wonder

Isn't she lovely,
Isn't she wonderful?
Isn't she precious,
Less than one minute old?
I never thought through love we'd be
Making one as lovely as she.
But isn't she lovely, made from love?

Isn't she pretty,
Truly the angels' best?
Boy, I'm so happy,
We have been heaven blessed.
I can't believe what God has done,
Through us He's given life to one.
But isn't she lovely, made from love?

Isn't she lovely?
Life and love are the same.
Life is Aisha,
The meaning of her name.
Londie, it could have not been done
Without you who conceived the one.
That's so very lovely, made from love.

It's My Turn

Words by Carole Bayer Sager
Music by Michael Masser

from the film *It's My Turn*
recorded by Diana Ross

I can't cover up my feelings in the name of love,
Or play it safe, for a while that was easy;
And if living for myself is what I'm guilty of,
Go on and sentence me, I'll still be free.

It's my turn to see what I can see.
I hope you'll understand this time's just for me,
Because it's my turn, with no apologies.
I've given up the truth to those I've tried to please,
But now it's my turn.
If I don't have all the answers,
At least I know I'll take my share of chances.

Ain't no use in holdin' on when nothing stays the same,
So I'll let it rain, 'cause the rain ain't gonna hurt me.
And I'll let you go, though I know it won't be easy.
It's my turn, with no more room for lies.
For years I've seen my life through someone else's eyes.
And now it's my turn to try and find my way.
And if I should get lost, at least I'll own today.
It's my turn, yes, it's my turn.

And there ain't no use in holdin' on when nothing stays the same,
So I'll let it rain, 'cause the rain ain't gonna hurt me.
And I'll let you go, though I know it won't be easy.
It's my turn, to see what I can see.
I hope you'll understand, this time's just for me.
Because it's my turn to turn and say good-bye.
I sure would like to know that you're still on my side,
Because it's my turn, it's my turn.

It's Too Late

Words by Toni Stern
Music by Carole King

recorded by Carole King

Stayed in bed all mornin' just to pass the time.
There's somethin' wrong here, there can be no denyin'.
One of us is changin' or maybe we've just stopped tryin'.

Refrain:
And it's too late, baby now, it's too late,
Though we really did try to make it.
Somethin' inside has died and I can't hide
And I just can't fake it.

It used to be so easy living here with you.
You were light and breezy and I knew just what to do.
Now you look so unhappy and I feel like a fool.

Refrain

There'll be good times again for me and you,
But we just can't stay together, don't you feel it too?
Still I'm glad for what we had and how I once loved you.

Refrain

It's too late, baby, it's too late
Now, darlin', it's too late.

Just My Imagination (Running Away with Me)

Words and Music by Norman J. Whitfield and Barrett Strong

recorded by The Temptations

Each day through my window I watch her as she passes by.
I say to myself: "You are such a lucky guy."
To have a girl like her is truly a dream come true.
Out of all the fellows in the world, she belongs to me.

Refrain:
But it was just my imagination
Runnin' away with me.
It was just my imagination
Runnin' away with me.

Soon, soon we'll be married and raise a family.
A cozy little home out in the country with children,
Maybe three.
I tell you I can visualize it all.
This couldn't be a dream, for too real it all seems.

Refrain

Every night on my knees I pray
"Dear Lord, hear my plea.
Don't ever let another take her love from me,
Or I would surely die."

Her love is heavenly.
When her arms enfold me,
I hear a tender Rhapsody.
But in reality,
She doesn't even know me.

Just my imagination
Runnin' away with me.
It was just my imagination
Runnin' away with me…

Just Once

Words by Cynthia Weil
Music by Barry Mann

recorded by Quincy Jones featuring James Ingram

I did my best,
But I guess my best wasn't good enough;
'Cause here we are,
Back where we were before.
Seems nothing ever changes,
We're back to being strangers,
Wondering if we ought to stay
Or head out the door.

Just once,
Can't we figure out what we keep
    doing wrong;
Why we never last for very long.
What are we doing wrong?
Just once,
Can't we find a way to finally make it right;
To make magic last for more than just
    one night?
If we could get to it,
I know we could break through it.

I gave it my all,
But I think my all may have been
    too much;
'Cause Lord knows we're not getting
    anywhere.
It seems we're always blowin'
Whatever we've got goin'.
And it seems at times with all we've got,
We haven't got a prayer.

Just once,
Can't we figure out what we keep
    doing wrong;
Why we never last for very long?
What are we doin' wrong?
Just once,
Can't we find a way to finally make it right?
To make the magic last for more than
    just one night?
I know we could get through it,
If we could just get to it.

Just once,
I want to understand;
Why it always comes back to goodbye.
Why can't we get ourselves in hand,
And admit to one another
We're no good without each other.
Take the best and make it better.
Find a way to stay together.

Just once,
Can't we find a way to finally make it right;
Oh, to make the magic last for more than
    just one night?
I know we could break through it,
If we could just get to it, just once.
Whoa, we can get to it, just once.

Killing Me Softly with His Song

Words by Norman Gimbel
Music by Charles Fox

recorded by Roberta Flack

Refrain:
Strummin' my pain with his fingers,
Singin' my life with his words.
Killing me softly with his song,
Killing me softly with his song,
Tellin' my whole life with his words,
Killing me softly with his song.

I heard he sang a good song,
And I heard he had a style,
And so I went to see him
And listen for a while.
And there he was, this stranger,
There before my eyes.

Refrain

I felt all flushed with fever,
Embarrassed by the crowd.
I felt he found my letters
And read each one out loud.
I prayed that he would finish,
But he just kept right on.

Refrain

He sang as if he knew me
In all my dark despair.
And then he looked right through me
As if I wasn't there.
And he just kept on singing,
Singing clear and strong.

Refrain

Laughter in the Rain

Words and Music by Neil Sedaka and Phil Cody

recorded by Neil Sedaka

Strolling along country roads with my baby,
It starts to rain, it begins to pour.
Without an umbrella we're soaked to the skin,
I feel a shiver run up my spine.
I feel the warmth of her hand in mine.

Refrain:
Oo, I hear laughter in the rain,
Walking hand in hand with the one I love.
Oo, how I love the rainy days
And the happy way I feel inside.

After a while we run under a tree,
I turn to her and she kisses me.
There with the beat of the rain on the leaves,
Softly she breathes and I close my eyes,
Sharing our love under stormy skies.

Refrain

Let It Be

Words and Music by John Lennon and Paul McCartney

recorded by The Beatles

When I find myself in times of trouble
Mother Mary comes to me
Speaking words of wisdom
Let it be.

And in my hour of darkness
She is standing right in front of me
Speaking words of wisdom
Let it be.

Let it be, let it be, let it be, let it be
Whisper words of wisdom
Let it be.

And when the broken-hearted people
Living in the world agree
There will be an answer
Let it be.

For though they may be parted there is
Still a chance that they will see
There will be an answer
Let it be.

Let it be, let it be, let it be, let it be
There will be an answer
Let it be.

And when the night is cloudy
There is still a light that shines on me
Shine until tomorrow
Let it be.

I wake up to the sound of music
Mother Mary comes to me
Speaking words of wisdom
Let it be.

Let it be, let it be, let it be, let it be
There will be an answer
Let it be.

Let it be, let it be, let it be, let it be
Whisper words of wisdom
Let it be...

The Living Years

Words and Music by Mike Rutherford and B.A. Robertson

recorded by Mike & The Mechanics

Every generation
Blames the one before,
And all of their frustrations
Come beating on your door.
I know that I'm a pris'ner
To all my father held so dear;
I know that I'm a hostage
To all his hopes and fears.
I just wish I could have told him
In the living years.

Oh, crumpled bits of paper
Filled with imperfect thought,
Stilted conversations,
I'm afraid that's all we've got.
You say you just don't see it,
He says it's perfect sense.
You just can't get agreement
In this present tense.
We all talk a diff'rent language,
Talking in defense.

Refrain:
Say it loud, say it clear,
You can listen as well as you hear.
It's too late when we die
To admit we don't see eye to eye.

So we open up a quarrel
Between the present and the past.
We only sacrifice the future;
It's the bitterness that lasts.
So don't yield to the fortunes
You sometimes see as fate.
It may have a new perspective
On a different day.
And if you don't give up
And don't give in,
You may just be OK.

Refrain

I wasn't there that morning
When my father passed away.
I didn't get to tell him
All the things I had to say.
I think I caught his spirit
Later that same year.
I'm sure I heard his echo
In my baby's newborn tears.
I just wish I could have told him
In the living years.

Refrain

The Long and Winding Road

Words and Music by John Lennon and Paul McCartney

recorded by The Beatles

The long and winding road that leads to your door,
Will never disappear, I've seen that road before.
It always leads me here, leads me to your door.

The wild and windy night that the rain washed away,
Has left a pool of tears crying for the day.
Why leave me standing here, let me know the way.

Many times I've been alone and many times I've cried,
Anyway, you'll never know the many ways I've tried.
But still they lead me back to the long and winding road.

You left me standing here a long, long time ago.
Don't leave me waiting here, lead me to you door.
Da da, da da …

Look What You've Done to Me

Words and Music by Boz Scaggs and David Foster

recorded by Boz Scaggs

Hope they never end this song.
This could take us all night long.
I looked at the moon and I felt blue.
Then I looked again and I saw you.
Eyes like fire in the night,
Bridges burning with their light.
Now I'll have to spend the whole night through,
And honey, yes, I'll have to spend it all on you.

Refrain:
Love, look what you've done to me.
Never thought I'd fall again so easily.
Oh, love, you wouldn't lie to me,
Leading me to feel this way.

They might fade and turn to stone.
Let's get crazy all alone.
Hold me closer than you'd ever dare.
Close your eyes and I'll be there.
And after all is said and done,
After all, you are the one.
Take me up your stairs and through the door.
Take me where we don't care anymore.

Refrain

Looks Like We Made It

Words and Music by Richard Kerr and Will Jennings

recorded by Barry Manilow

There you are,
Lookin' just the same as you did the last time I touched you.
And here I am,
Close to gettin' tangled up inside the thought of you.
Do you love him as much as I love her?
And will that love be strong when old feelings start to stir?
Looks like we made it.

Refrain:
Left each other on the way to another love.
Looks like we made it,
Or I thought so till today, until you were there, everywhere,
And all I could taste was love the way we made it.

Love's so strange,
Playing hide and seek with hearts and always hurting.
And we're the fools,
Standing close enough to touch those burning memories.
And if I hold you for the sake of all those times
Love made us lose our minds,
Could I ever let you go?
Oh no, we've made it.

Refrain

Oh, we made it.
Looks like we made it.
Looks like we made it.

Lost in Your Eyes

Words and Music by Deborah Gibson

recorded by Debbie Gibson

I get lost in your eyes,
And I feel my spirits rise
And soar like the wind.
Is it love that I am in?

I get weak in a glance.
Isn't this what's called romance?
And now I know,
'Cause when I'm lost, I can't let go.

Refrain:
I don't mind not knowing
What I'm headed for.
You can take me to the skies.
It's like being lost in heaven
When I'm lost in your eyes.

I just fell, don't know why.
Something's there we can't deny.
And when I first knew
Was when I first looked at you.

And if I can't find my way,
If salvation seems worlds away,
Oh, I'll be found
When I am lost in your eyes.

Refrain

I get weak in a glance.
Isn't this what's called romance?
Oh, I'll be found
When I am lost in your eyes.

Love Takes Time

Words and Music by Mariah Carey and Ben Margulies

recorded by Mariah Carey

I had it all but I let it slip away.
Couldn't see I treated you wrong.
Now I wander around feeling down and cold,
Trying to believe that you're gone.

Refrain:
Love takes time to heal
When you're hurting so much.
Couldn't see that I was blind to let you go.
I can't escape the pain inside,
'Cause love takes time.
I don't want to be here.
I don't want to be here alone.

Losing my mind from this hollow in my heart.
Suddenly I'm so incomplete, yeah.
Lord, I'm needing you now.
Tell me how to stop the rain.
Tears are falling down endlessly.

Refrain

You might say that it's over.
You might say that you don't care.
You might say you don't miss me.
You don't need me.
But I know that you do
And I feel that you do inside.

Refrain

Love's Grown Deep

Words and Music by Kenny Nolan

recorded by Kenny Nolan

Somewhere back in time
You became a friend of mine,
And day by day we've grown a little closer.
You're my spirit to be strong,
A friend when things go wrong,
So I've written down these words to let you know.

Refrain:
Love's grown deep, deep into the heart of me.
You've become a part of me.
Let us plant a seed and watch it grow.
Love's grown deep, deep into the heart of me.
You've become a part of me.

As we travel down the road
Side by side, we'll share the load.
Hand in hand we'll see each other through.
Though we've only just begun,
Let's count our blessings one by one.
I thank God for life, I thank God for you.

Refrain

As the seasons slip away,
Forever lovers we will stay.
Together do or die with all our heart.

Refrain

Lullabye (Goodnight, My Angel)

Words and Music by Billy Joel

recorded by Billy Joel

Goodnight, my angel, time to close your eyes,
And save these questions for another day.
I think I know what you've been asking me.
I think you know what I've been trying to say.
I promised I would never leave you,
And you should always know
Wherever you may go,
No matter where you are,
I never will be far away.

Goodnight, my angel, now it's time to sleep,
And still so many things I want to say.
Remember all the songs you sang for me
When we went sailing on an emerald bay.
And like a boat out on the ocean,
I'm rocking you to sleep.
The water's dark and deep inside this ancient heart
You'll always be a part of me.

Goodnight, my angel, now it's time to dream,
And dream how wonderful your life will be.
Someday your child may cry,
And if you sing this lullaby,
Then in your heart there will always be a part of me.

Someday we'll all be gone
But lullabyes goes on and on.
They never die, that's how you and I will be.

Make It with You

Words and Music by David Gates

recorded by Bread

Hey, have you ever tried
Really reaching out for the other side?
I'm may be climbing on rainbows,
But baby, here goes.

Dreams, they're for those who sleep.
Life, it's for us to keep.
And if you're wondering
What this all is leading to,
I'd like to make it with you.
I really think that we could make it, girl.

No, you don't know me well,
And ev'ry little thing, only time will tell.
But you believe the things that I do
And we'll see it through.

Life can be short or long.
Love can be right or wrong.
And if I chose the one
I'd like to help me through,
I'd like to make it with you.
I really think that we can make it, girl.

Baby, you know that
Dreams, they're for those who sleep.
Life, it's for us to keep.
And if I chose the one
I'd like to help me through,
I'd like to make it with you.
I really think that we could make it, girl.

Mandy

Words and Music by Scott English and Richard Kerr

recorded by Barry Manilow

I remember all my life
Raining down as cold as ice.
Shadows of a man,
A face through a window,
Cryin' in the night,
The night goes into…

Morning's just another day;
Happy people pass my way.
Looking in their eyes,
I see a memory
I never realized
How happy you made me.

Refrain:
Oh, Mandy,
Well, you came and you gave
    without taking.
But I sent you away.
Oh, Mandy,
Well, you kissed me and stopped
    me from shaking,
And I need you today.
Oh, Mandy!

I'm standing on the edge of time;
I've walked away when love was mine.
Caught up in a world of up-hill climbing,
The tears are in my mind
And nothin' is rhyming,

Refrain

Yesterday's a dream,
I face the morning.
Crying on a breeze
The pain is calling.

Refrain

Oh, Mandy,
Well, you came and you gave
    without taking,
But I sent you away.
Oh, Mandy,
Well, you kissed me and stopped
    me from shaking,
And I need you.

Mercy, Mercy Me (The Ecology)

Words and Music by Marvin Gaye

recorded by Marvin Gaye

Woo, ah,
Mercy, mercy me.
Ah, things ain't what they used to be.
No, no, where did all the blue skies go,
Poison is the wind that blows
From the north and south and east.

Wo, mercy, mercy me.
Ah, things ain't what they used to be, no, no
Oil wasted on the ocean and upon
Our seas' fish full of mercury, Ah.

Oh, mercy, mercy me.
Ah things ain't what they used to be.
No, no, no, radiation underground and in the sky;
Animals and birds who live nearby are dying.

Oh, mercy, mercy me.
Ah things ain't what they used to be.
What about this overcrowded land?
How much more abuse from man can she stand?

Oh na, na,
My sweet Lord,
No, no, na, na, na,
My, my sweet Lord.

Midnight Blue

Words and Music by Carole Bayer Sager and Melissa Manchester

recorded by Melissa Manchester

Whenever it is, it'll keep till the morning.
Haven't we both got better things to do?
Midnight blue.
Even though simple things become rough,
Haven't we had enough?

Refrain:
And I think we can make it one more time.
If we try, one more time for all the old times.

For all of the times you told me you need me,
Needing me now is something I could use.
Midnight blue.
Wouldn't you give your hand to a friend?
Maybe it's not the end.

Refrain

Think we can make it, think we can make it.
Wouldn't you give your heart to a friend?
Think of me as your friend.
And I think we can make it.
And I think we can make it.

My Eyes Adored You

Words and Music by Bob Crewe and Kenny Nolan

recorded by Frankie Valli

Refrain:
My eyes adored you.
Though I never laid a hand on you,
My eyes adored you.
Like a million miles away from me
You couldn't see how I adored you.
So close, so close and yet so far.

Carried your books from school,
Playin' make believe you're married to me.
You were fifth grade, I was sixth,
When we came to be.
Walkin' home every day
Over Barnegat Bridge and bay,
Till we grew into the me and you
Who went our sep'rate ways.

Refrain

Headed for city lights,
Climbed the ladder up to fortune and fame.
Worked my fingers to the bone,
Made myself a name.
Funny, I seem to find
That no matter how the years unwind,
Still I reminisce 'bout the girl I miss
And the love I left behind.

Refrain

My Father's Eyes

Words and Music by Eric Clapton

recorded by Eric Clapton

Sailing down behind the sun,
Waiting for my prince to come.
Praying for the healing rain
To restore my soul again.

Just a toe rag on the run.
How did I get here?
What have I done?
When will all my hopes arise?
How will I know him
When I look in...

Refrain:
My father's eyes,
(Look into my father's eyes.)
My father's eyes.
When I look in my father's eyes.
(Look into my father's eyes.)
My father's eyes.

Then the light begins to shine
And I hear those ancient lullabies.
And as I watch this seedling grow,
Feel my heart start to overflow.

Where do I find the words to say?
How do I teach him?
What do we play?
Bit by bit I'd realize
That's when I need them
That's when I need them
That's when I need...

Refrain

Then the jagged edge appears
Through the distant clouds of tears.
And I'm like a bridge that was washed away.
My foundations were made of clay.

And as my soul slides down to die,
How could I lose him?
What did I try?
Bit by bit I'd realize
That he was here with me.
I looked into...

Refrain Twice

My Heart Belongs to Me

Words and Music by Alan Gordon

recorded by Barbra Streisand

I got the feelin' the feeling's gone,
My heart has gone to sleep.
One of these mornings I'll be gone.
My heart belongs to me.

Can we believe in fairy tales?
Can love survive when all else fails?
Can't hide the feelin' the feeling's gone.
My heart belongs to me.

But now my love, hey didn't I love you,
But we knew what had to be.
Somehow my love, I'll always love you,
But my heart belongs to me.

Put out the light and close your eyes,
Come lie beside me, don't ask why.
Can't hide the feelin' the feeling's gone.
My heart belongs to me.

(But now my love, hey didn't I love you?
Didn't I love you?
Didn't I love you?
Didn't I love you, baby?)

Don't cry, my love, I'll always love you,
But my heart belongs to me.
I got the feelin' the feeling's gone.
My heart belongs to me.

My Heart Will Go On (Love Theme from 'Titanic')

Music by James Horner
Lyric by Will Jennings

from the Paramount and Twentieth Century Fox Motion Picture *Titanic*
recorded by Celine Dion

Every night in my dreams I see you, I feel you.
That is how I know you go on.
Far across the distance and spaces between us
You have come to show you go on.

Refrain:
Near, far, wherever you are,
I believe that the heart does go on.
Once more you open the door
And you're here in my heart,
And my heart will go on and on.

Love can touch us one time
And last for a lifetime,
And never let go till we're gone.
Love was when I loved you;
One true time I hold to.
In my life we'll always go on.

Refrain

You're here, there's nothing I fear
And I know that my heart will go on.
We'll stay forever this way.
You are safe in my heart,
And my heart will go on and on.

New York State of Mind

Words and Music by Billy Joel

recorded by Billy Joel

Some folks like to get away,
Take a holiday
From the neighborhood,
Hop a flight to Miami Beach or to
    Hollywood.
But I'm takin' a Greyhound on the
    Hudson River line.
I'm in a New York state of mind.

I've seen all the movie stars
In their fancy cars
And their limousines,
Been high in the Rockies under the
    evergreens.
But I know what I'm needin',
And I don't want to waste more time.
I'm in a New York state of mind.

Refrain:
It was so easy livin' day by day,
Out of touch with the rhythm and blues.
And now I need a little give and take.
The *New York Times* and the *Daily News*.

Comes down to reality,
And it's fine with me 'cause I've let it slide.
Don't care if it's Chinatown or on Riverside.
I don't have any reasons.
I've left them all behind.
I'm in a New York state of mind.

Refrain

Repeat Verse 3

I don't have any reasons.
I've left them all behind.
I'm in a New York state of mind.

The Next Time I Fall

Words and Music by Paul Gordon and Bobby Caldwell

recorded by Peter Cetera with Amy Grant

Love, like a road that never ends.
How it leads me back again
To heartache,
I'll never understand.
Darling, I put my heart upon the shelf
'Til the moment was right. And I tell myself

Refrain:
Next time I fall in love
I'll know better what to do.
Next time I fall in love,
Ooh, Ooh, Ooh.
The next time I fall in love,
The next time I fall in love
It will be with you.

Oh, now, as I look into your eyes,
Well, I wonder if it's wise
To hold you like I've wanted to before.

Tonight, ooh, I was thinking that you might
Be the one who breathes life in this heart of mine.

Refrain

(It will be with you.)
Next time I'm gonna follow through.
And if it drives me crazy,
I will know better why
The next time I try.

Refrain Twice

On and On

Words and Music by Stephen Bishop

recorded by Stephen Bishop

Down in Jamaica they got lots of pretty women.
Steal your money, then they break your heart.
Lonesome Sue, she's in love with ol' Sam.
Take him from the fire into the frying pan.

On and on, she just keeps on trying,
And she smiles when she feels like crying.
On and on, on and on, on and on.

Poor ol' Jimmy sits alone in the moonlight.
Saw his woman kiss another man.
So he takes a ladder, steals the stars from the sky,
Puts on Sinatra and starts to cry.

On and on, he just keeps on trying,
And he smiles when he feels like crying.
On and on, on and on, on and on.

When the first time is the last time,
It can make you feel so bad.
But if you know it, show it.
Hold on tight. Don't let her say goodnight.

Got the sun on my shoulders and my toes in the sand.
My woman's left me for some other man.
Ah, but I don't care. I'll just dream and stay tan.
Toss up my heart to see where it lands.

On and on, I just keep on trying,
And I smile when I feel like dying.
On and on, on and on, on and on.
On and on, on and on, on and on.
On and on, on and on, on and on.

One Day I'll Fly Away

Words and Music by Will Jennings and Joe Sample

from the film *Moulin Rouge*
recorded by Nicole Kidman

I follow the night,
Can't stand the light.
When will I begin to live again?

One day I'll fly away,
Leave all this to yesterday.
What more could your love do for me?
When will love be through with me?
Why live life from dream to dream,
And dread the day when dreaming ends?

One day I'll fly away,
Leave all this to yesterday.
Why live life from dream to dream,
And dread the day when dreaming ends?

One day I'll fly away,
Fly, fly away.

One Less Bell to Answer

Lyric by Hal David
Music by Burt Bacharach

recorded by The 5th Dimension

One less bell to answer.
One less egg to fry.
One less man to pick up after.
I should be happy, but all I do is cry.

Group:
Cry, cry,
No more laughter.

Solo:
I should be happy.

Group:
Oh, why did he go?

Solo:
Oh, I only know that since he left
My life's so empty.
Though I try to forget,
It just can't be done.
Each time the doorbell rings
I still run.

I don't know how in the world
To stop thinking of him
'Cause I still love him so.
I end each day the way I start out,
Cryin' my heart out.

One less bell to answer.
One less egg to fry.
One less man to pick up after.
No more laughter,
No more love
Since he went away.

Group:
Ah, ah, ah...

One More Night

Words and Music by Phil Collins

recorded by Phil Collins

I've been trying for so long
To let you know,
Let you know how I feel,
And if I stumble, if I fall
Just help me back,
So I can make you see.

Please give me one more night,
Give me one more night.
One more night,
'Cause I can't wait forever.
Give me just one more night,
Oh, just one more night,
Oh, one more night,
'Cause I can't wait forever.

I've been sitting here so long
Wasting time,
Just staring at the phone,
And I was wondering should I call you
Then I thought,
Maybe you're not alone.

Please give me one more night,
Give me just one more night,
One more night.
'Cause I can't wait forever.
Please give me one more night,
Oh, just one more night,
Oh, one more night,
'Cause I can't wait forever.

Give me one more night,
Give me just one more night,
Just one more night
'Cause I can't wait forever.

Like a river to the sea,
I will always be with you,
And if you sail away
I will follow you.
Give me one more night,
Give me just one more night,
Oh, one more night
'Cause I can't wait forever.

I know there'll never be a time
You'll ever feel the same,
And I know it's only right.
But if you change your mind,
You know that I'll be here,
And maybe we both can learn.

Give me just one more night,
Give me just one more night.
One more night,
'Cause I can't wait forever.
Give me just one more night,
Give me just one more night,
Oh, one more night,
'Cause I can't wait forever.

Ooh, ooh, ooh...

One Sweet Day

Words and Music by Mariah Carey, Walter Afanasieff, Shawn Stockman,
Michael McCary, Nathan Morris and Wanya Morris

recorded by Mariah Carey & Boyz II Men

Sorry I never told you
All I wanted to say.
And now it's too late to hold you,
'Cause you've flown away,
So far away.

Never had I imagined
Living without your smile.
Feeling and knowing you hear me,
It keeps me alive,
Alive.

Refrain:
And I know you're shining down on me from heaven,
Like so many friends we've lost along the way.
And I know eventually we'll be together
One sweet day.

Darling, I never showed you,
Assumed you'd always be there.
I, I took your presence for granted,
But I always cared,
And I miss the love we shared.

Refrain

The One That You Love

Words and Music by Graham Russell

recorded by Air Supply

Now the night has gone;
Now the night has gone away;
Doesn't seem that long;
We hardly had two words to say.
Hold me in your arms for just another day,
I promise this one will go slow;
Oh, we have the right you know;
We have the right you know.

Don't say the morning's come;
Don't say the morning's come so soon.
Must we end this way,
When so much here is hard to lose?
Love is everywhere;
I know it is;
Such moments as this are too few;
Oh, it's all up to you;
It's all up to you.

Refrain:
Here I am,
The one that you love,
Asking for another day;
Understand, the one that you love,
Loves you in so many ways.

Tell me we can stay.
Tell me we can stay, oh please.
They are the words to say,
The only words I can believe.
Hold me in your arms for just another day,
I promise this one will go slow;
Oh, we have the right you know;
We have the right you know.

Refrain Twice

Repeat and Fade:
The night has gone,
A part of yesterday;
I don't know what to say;
I don't know what to say.
Here I am,
The one that you love,
Asking for another day;
Understand, the one that you love,
Loves you in so many ways.

Only Yesterday

Words and Music by Richard Carpenter and John Bettis

recorded by The Carpenters

After long enough of being alone,
Ev'ryone must face their share
   of loneliness.
In my own time, nobody knew
The pain I was goin' through,
And waitin' was all my heart could do.

Hope was all I had until you came.
Maybe you can't see how much you
   mean to me.
You were the dawn breaking the night,
The promise of morning light,
Filling the world surrounding me.

Refrain:
And when I hold you, baby, baby,
Feels like maybe things will be alright.
Baby, baby, your love's made me
Free as a song, singin' forever.
Only yesterday when I was sad and
   I was lonely,
You showed me the way to leave the past
And all its tears behind me.
Tomorrow may be even brighter
   than today,
Since I threw my sadness away,
Only yesterday.

I have found my home here in your arms;
Nowhere else on earth I'd really rather be.
Life waits for us; share it with me.
The best is about to be,
And so much is left for us to see.

Refrain

Only yesterday when I was sad and
   I was lonely,
You showed me the way to leave the past
And all its tears behind me.
Tomorrow may be even brighter
   than today,
Since I threw my sadness away,
Only yesterday.

Operator (That's Not the Way It Feels)

Words and Music by Jim Croce

recorded by Jim Croce

Operator,
Could you help me place this call?
You see, the number on the match book
   is old and faded.
She's living in L.A.
With my best old ex-friend, Ray,
A guy she said she knew well and
   sometimes hated.

Refrain:
Isn't that the way they say it goes?
But let's forget all that,
And give me the number, if you can find it,
So I can call just to tell them I'm fine
   and to show
I've overcome the blow,
I've learned to take it well.
I only wish my words could just
   convince myself
That it wasn't real,
But that's not the way it feels.

Operator,
Could you help me place this call,
'Cause I can't read the number that
   you just gave me.
There's something in my eyes;
You know it happens every time
I think about the love that I thought
   would save me.

Refrain

Operator,
Let's forget about this call;
There's no one there I really wanted
   to talk to.
Thank you for your time
'Cause you've been so much more than kind,
And you can keep the dime.

Refrain

Our House

Words and Music by Graham Nash

recorded by Crosby, Stills, Nash & Young

I'll light the fire;
You place the flowers in the vase
That you bought today.
Staring at the fire
For hours and hours
While I listen to you play your love songs
All night long for me,
Only for me.

Come to me now
And rest your head for just five minutes;
Everything is done.

Such a cozy room.
The windows are illuminated
By the evening sunshine through them:
Fiery gems for you,
Only for you.

Refrain:
Our house
Is a very, very, very fine house,
With two cats in the yard.
Life used to be so hard;
Now everything is easy 'cause of you.
And, ah.

La la la…

Refrain

And, ah,
I'll light the fire,
While you place the flowers in the vase
That you bought today.

Poetry Man

Words and Music by Phoebe Snow

recorded by Phoebe Snow

You make me laugh,
'Cause your eyes, they light the night,
They look right through me.
La la la la.
You bashful boy,
You're hiding something sweet;
Please give it to me, yeah, to me.

Refrain:
Oh, talk to me some more.
You don't have to go.
You're the Poetry Man.
You make things all rhyme.

You are a genie.
All I ask for is your smile
Each time I rub the lamp.
La la la la.
When I am with you
I have a giggling teen-age crush,
Though I'm a sultry vamp, yeah, a sultry vamp.

Refrain

So once again,
It's time to say so long
And so recall the lull of life.
La la la la.
You're going home now.
Home's that place somewhere
You go each day to see your wife, yeah.

Refrain

The Rainbow Connection

Words and Music by Paul Williams and Kenneth L. Ascher

from the film *The Muppet Movie*

Why are there so many songs about rainbows,
And what's on the other side?
Rainbows are visions, but only illusions,
And rainbows have nothing to hide.
So we've been told, and some choose not to believe it;
I know they're wrong; wait and see
Someday we'll find it,
The rainbow connection;
The lovers, the dreamers, and me.

Who said that every wish would be heard and answered
When wished on the morning star?
Somebody thought of that, and someone believed it;
Look what it's done so far.
What's so amazing that keeps us star-gazing
And what do we think we might we might see?
Someday we'll find it,
The rainbow connection;
The lovers, the dreamers, and me.

All of us under its spell;
We know that it's probably magic.
Have you been half asleep and have you heard voices?
I've heard them calling my name.

Is this the sweet sound that calls the young sailors?
The voice might be one and the same.
I've heard it too many times to ignore it.
It's something that I'm supposed to be.
Someday we'll find it,
The rainbow connection;
The lovers, the dreamers, and me.

Rainy Days and Mondays

Lyrics by Paul Williams
Music by Roger Nichols

recorded by The Carpenters

Talkin' to myself and feelin' old,
Sometimes I'd like to quit.
Nothing ever seems to fit.
Hangin' around, nothing to do but frown;
Rainy days and Mondays always get
   me down.

What I've got they used to call the blues,
Nothing is really wrong,
Feelin' like I don't belong.
Walkin' around, some kind of
   lonely clown;
Rainy days and Mondays always get
   me down.

Refrain:
Funny but it seems I always wind up here
   with you,
Nice to know somebody loves me.
Funny but it seems that it's the only
   thing to do,
Run and find the one who loves me.

What I feel has come and gone before,
No need to talk it out,
We know what it's all about.
Hangin' around, nothing to do but frown;
Rainy days and Mondays always get
   me down.

Refrain

What I feel has come and gone before,
No need to talk it out,
We know what it's all about.
Hangin' around, nothing to do but frown;
Rainy days and Mondays always get
   me down.
Hangin' around, nothing to do but frown;
Rainy days and Mondays always get
   me down.
Rainy days and Mondays always get
   me down.

Reach Out and Touch (Somebody's Hand)

Words and Music by Nickolas Ashford and Valerie Simpson

recorded by Diana Ross

Refrain:
Reach out and touch somebody's hand,
Make this world a better place if you can.
Reach out and touch somebody's hand,
Make this world a better place if you can.
(Just try)

Take a little time out of your busy day,
To give encouragement to someone who's lost the way.
Or would I be talking to a stone
If I asked you to share a problem that's not your own.
We can change things if we start giving.

Refrain

If you see an old friend on the street
And he's down, remember, his shoes could fit your feet.
Just try a little kindness and you'll see
It's something that comes very naturally.
We can change things if we start giving.

Why don't you
Reach out and touch somebody's hand.

Ready to Take a Chance Again (Love Theme)

Words by Norman Gimbel
Music by Charles Fox

from the Paramount Picture *Foul Play*
recorded by Barry Manilow

You remind me I live in a shell,
Safe from the past, and doin' okay,
But not very well.

No jolts, no surprises, no crisis arises.
My life goes along as it should.
It's all very nice, but not very good.

And I'm ready to take a chance again,
Ready to put my love on the line with you.
Been living with nothing to show for it.
You get what you get when you go for it,
And I'm ready to take a chance again with you.

When she left me in all my despair,
I just held on. My hopes were all gone,
Then I found you there.

And I'm ready to take a chance again,
Ready to put my love on the line with you.
Been living with nothing to show for it.
You get what you get when you go for it,
And I'm ready to take a chance again,
Ready to take a chance again with you,
With you.

Reflection

Music by Matthew Wilder
Lyrics by David Zippel

from Walt Disney Pictures' *Mulan*
recorded by Christina Aguilera

Look at me,
You may think you see who I really am,
But you'll never know me.
Every day it's as if I play a part.

Now I see if I wear a mask I can fool the world,
But I cannot fool my heart.
Who is that girl I see staring straight back at me?
When will my reflection show who I am am inside?
I am now in a world where I have to hide my heart
And what I believe in.

But somehow I will show the world
What's inside my heart and be loved for who I am.
Who is that girl I see staring straight back at me?
Why is my reflection someone I don't know?
Must I pretend that I'm someone else for all time?
When will my reflection show who I am?
Inside, there's a heart that must be free to fly,
That burns with a need to know the reason why.

Why must we all conceal what we think, how we feel?
Must there be a secret me I'm forced to hide?
I won't pretend that I'm someone else for all time.
When will my reflection show who I am inside?
When will my reflection show who I am inside?

Remember Me This Way

Music by David Foster
Lyrics by Linda Thompson

from the Universal Motion Picture *Casper*
recorded by Jordan Hill

Every now and then
We find a special friend
Who never lets us down,
Who understands it all,
Reaches out each time you fall.
You're the best friend that I've found.

I know you can't stay,
But part of you will never, ever go away;
Your heart will stay.

Refrain:
I'll make a wish for you and hope it
  will come true:
That life will just be kind to such a
  gentle mind.
If you lose your way, think back on
  yesterday.
Remember me this way.
Remember me this way.

I don't need eyes to see
The love you bring to me,
No matter where I go.

And I know that you'll be there,
Forevermore a part of me;
You're everywhere.
I'll always care.

Refrain

And I'll be right behind your shoulder watch-
  ing you.
I'll be standing by your side in all you do.
And I won't ever leave,
As long as you believe.
You just believe.

Refrain

This way.

Rocky Mountain High

Words by John Denver
Music by John Denver and Mike Taylor

recorded by John Denver

He was born in the summer of his
   twenty-seventh year,
Comin' home to a place he'd never
   been before.
He left yesterday behind him,
You might say he was born again,
You might say he found a key for
   every door.

When he first came to the mountains
   his life was far away,
On the road and hangin' by a song.
But the string's already broken and
   doesn't really care,
It keeps changin' fast and it don't last
   for long.

But the Colorado Rocky Mountain high
I've seen it rainin' fire in the sky.
The shadow from the starlight
Is softer than a lullaby.
Rocky Mountain high,
Rocky Mountain high.

He climbed cathedral mountains,
He saw silver clouds below,
He saw everything as far as you can see.
And they say that he got crazy once
And tried to touch the sun,
And he lost a friend but kept a memory.

Now he walks in quiet solitude, the forests
   and the streams
Seeking grace in every step he takes.
His sight has turned inside himself to try
   and understand
The serenity of a clear blue mountain lake.

And the Colorado Rocky Mountain high,
I've seen it rainin' fire in the sky.
Talk to God and listen to the casual reply.
Rocky Mountain high.

Now his life is full of wonder
But his heart still knows some fear
Of a simple thing he cannot comprehend.
Why they try to tear the mountains down
To bring in a couple more
More people, more scars upon the land.

And the Colorado Rocky Mountain high,
I've seen it rainin' fire in the sky.
I know he'd be a poorer man if he never saw
   an eagle fly.
Rocky Mountain high

It's a Colorado Rocky Mountain high,
I've seen it rainin' fire in the sky.
Friends around the campfire
And everybody's high.
Rocky Mountain high…

Sailing

Words and Music by Christopher Cross

recorded by Christopher Cross

Well, it's not far down to paradise,
At least it's not for me.
And if the wind is right you can sail away
And find tranquility.
Oh, the canvas can do miracles,
Just you wait and see.
Believe me.

It's not far to never-never-land,
No reason to pretend.
And if the wind is right you can find the joy
Of innocence again.
Oh, the canvas can do miracles,
Just you wait and see.
Believe me.

Refrain:
Sailing,
Takes me away,
To where I've always heard it could be.
Just a dream and the wind to carry me,
And soon I will be free.

Fantasy,
It gets the best of me
When I'm sailing.

All caught up in the reverie,
Every word is a symphony.
Won't you believe me?

Refrain

Well, it's not far back to reality,
At least it's not for me.
And if the wind is right you can sail away,
And find serenity.
Oh, the canvas can do miracles,
Just you wait and see.
Believe me.

Refrain

Same Old Lang Syne

Words and Music by Dan Fogelberg

recorded by Dan Fogelberg

Met my old lover in the groc'ry store.
The snow was falling, Christmas Eve.
I stole behind her in the frozen foods
And I touched her on the sleeve.

She didn't recognize the face at first,
But then her eyes flew open wide.
She went to hug me and she spilled
   her purse,
And we laughed until we cried.

We took her groc'ries to the
   checkout stand;
The food was totaled up and bagged.
We stood there, lost in our embarrassment,
As the conversation lagged.

We went to have ourselves a drink or two,
But couldn't find an open bar.
We bought a six-pack at the liquor store
And we drank it in her car.

Refrain:
We drank a toast to innocence;
We drank a toast to now.
We tried to reach beyond the emptiness,
But neither one knew how.

She said she'd married her an architect,
Who kept her warm and safe and dry.
She would have liked to say she loved
   the man,
But she didn't like to lie.

I said the years had been a friend to her
And that her eyes were still as blue.
But in those eyes I wasn't sure if I
Saw doubt or gratitude.

She said she saw me in the record stores
And that I must be doing well.
I said the audience was heavenly,
But the traveling was hell.

Refrain

We drank a toast to innocence,
We drank a toast to time,
Reliving in our eloquence
Another "Auld Lang Syne."

The beer was empty and our tongues
   were tired
And running out of things to say.
She gave a kiss to me as I got out
And I watched her drive away.

Just for a moment I was back at school
And felt that old familiar pain.
And as I turned to make my way back home,
The snow turned into rain.

Saving All My Love for You

Words by Gerry Goffin
Music by Michael Masser

recorded by Whitney Houston

A few stolen moments is all that we share.
You've got your family and they need you there.
Though I try to resist,
Being last on you list,
But no other man's gonna do,
So I'm saving all my love for you.

It's not very easy living all alone.
My friends try and tell me find a man of my own.
But each time I try,
I just break down and cry.
'Cause I'd rather be home feelin' blue,
So I'm saving all my love for you.

You used to tell me we'd run away together;
Love gives you the right to be free.
You said: "Be patient. Just wait a little longer,"
But that's just an old fantasy.
I've got to get ready, just a few minutes more.
Gonna get that old feelin' when you walk through that door.
'Cause tonight is the night for feeling all right.
We'll be making love the whole night through,
So I'm saving my love,
Yes I'm saving my love,
Yes I'm saving all my love for you.

No other woman is gonna love you more.
'Cause tonight is the night that I'm feeling all right.
We'll be making love the whole night through;
So I'm saving all my love,
Yes, I'm saving all my loving,
Yes I'm saving all my love for you.
For you.

Separate Lives

Words and Music by Stephen Bishop

Love Theme from *White Nights*
recorded by Phil Collins & Marilyn Martin

You called me from the room in your hotel
All full of romance for someone you had met,
And telling me how sorry you were,
Leaving so soon,
And that you miss me sometimes
When you're alone in your room.
Do I feel lonely too?

You have no right to ask me how I feel.
You have no right to speak to me so kind.
I can't go on holding onto ties
Now that we're living
Sep'rate lives.

Well, I held on to let you go.
And if you lost your love for me,
You never let it show.
There was no way to compromise.
So now we're livin'
Separate lives.

Oh, it's so typical;
Love leads to isolation.
So you build that wall,
So you build that wall
And make it stronger.

You have no right to ask me how I feel.
You have no right to speak to me so kind.
Someday I might find myself looking in your eyes.
But for now we'll go on living separate lives.
Yes, for now we'll go on
Living separate lives.

She's Always a Woman

Words and Music by Billy Joel

recorded by Billy Joel

She can kill with a smile.
She can wound with her eyes.
She can ruin your faith
With her casual lies.
And she only reveals
What she wants you to see.
She hides like a child,
But she's always a woman to me.

She can lead you to love,
She can take you or leave you.
She can ask for the truth,
But she'll never believe you,
And she'll take what you give her
As long as it's free,
Yeah, she steals like a thief,
But she's always a woman to me.

Refrain:
Oh, she takes care of herself,
She can wait if she wants,
She's ahead of her time.
Oh, and she never gives out
And she never gives in,
She just changes her mind.

And she'll promise you more
Than the garden of Eden.
Then she'll carelessly cut you
And laugh while you're bleedin'.
But she brings out the best
And the worst you can be,
Blame it all on yourself
'Cause she's always a woman to me.

Refrain

She is frequently kind
And she's suddenly cruel.
She can do as she pleases,
She's nobody's fool.
But she can't be convicted,
She's earned her degree.
And the most she will do
Is throw shadows at you,
But she's always a woman to me.

She's Got a Way

Words and Music by Billy Joel

recorded by Billy Joel

She's got a way about her.
I don't know what it is,
But I know that I can't live without her.
She's got a way of pleasin'.
I don't know what it is,
But there doesn't have to be a reason anywhere.

She's got a smile that heals me.
I don't know what it is,
But I have to laugh when she reveals me.
She's got a way of talkin'.
I don't know what it is,
But it lifts me up when we are walkin' anywhere.

She comes to me when I'm feelin' down,
Inspires me without a sound.
She touches me and I get turned around.
She's got a way of showin' how I make her feel,
And I find the strength to keep on goin'.

She's got a light around her,
And everywhere she goes,
A million dreams of love surround her everywhere.
She comes to me when I'm feelin' down,
Inspires me without a sound.
She touches me, I get turned around.
Oh, oh, oh.

She's got a smile that heals me.
I don't know why it is,
But I have to laugh when she reveals me.
She's got a way about her.
I don't know what it is,
But I know that I can't live without her anyway.

Sing

Words and Music by Joe Raposo

from the television show *Sesame Street*
recorded by The Carpenters

Sing, sing a song.
Sing out loud, sing out strong.
Sing of good things, not bad.
Sing of happy, not sad.

Sing, sing a song,
Make it simple, to last your whole life long.
Don't worry that it's not good enough
For anyone else to hear;
Just sing, sing a song.

La la la la la,
La la la la la la,
La la la la la la la.

Sing, sing a song.
Let the world sing along.
Sing of love there could be.
Sing for you and for me.

Sing, sing a song.
Make it simple, to last your whole life long.
Don't worry that it's not good enough
For anyone else to hear;
Just sing, sing a song.
Just sing, sing a song.
Just sing, sing a song.

La la la la la,
La la la la la la,
La la la la la la la.

So Far Away

Words and Music by Carole King

recorded by Carole King

So far away!
Doesn't anybody stay in one place anymore?
It would be so fine to see your face at my door.
Doesn't help to know that you're just time away.
Long ago, I reached for you and there you stood.
Holding you again could only do me good.
How I wish I could, but you're so far away!

One more song about movin' along the highway.
Can't say much of anything that's new.
If I could only work this life out my way,
I'd rather spend it bein' close to you.
But you're so…

Repeat Verse 1

Yeah, you're so far away!
Travelin' around sure gets me down and lonely.
Nothin' else to do but close my mind.
I sure hope the road don't come to own me.
There's so many dreams I've yet to find.
But you're so far away!

Repeat Verses 1 and 2 and Fade

Solitaire

Words and Music by Neil Sedaka and Phil Cody

recorded by The Carpenters

There was a man, a lonely man
Who lost his love through his indifference.
A heart that cared, that went unshared
Until it died within his silence.

Refrain:
And solitare's the only game in town.
And ev'ry road that takes him takes him down.
And by himself it's easy to pretend
He'll never love again.
And keeping to himself he plays the game.
Without her love it always ends the same.
While life goes on around him ev'rywhere,
He's playing solitaire.

A little hope goes up in smoke.
Just how it goes, goes without saying.
There was a man, a lonely man
Who would command the hand he's playing.

Refrain

And solitare's the only game in town.
And ev'ry road that takes him takes him down.
While life goes on around him ev'rywhere,
He's playing solitaire.

Something About the Way You Look Tonight

Words and Music by Elton John and Bernie Taupin

recorded by Elton John

There was a time I was everything and nothing all in one.
When you found me, I was feeling like a cloud across the sun.

Well, I need to tell you how you light up every second of the day,
But in the moonlight, you just shine like a beacon of the bay.

Refrain:
I can't explain,
But there's something about the way you look tonight,
Takes my breath away.
It's that feeling I get about you deep inside.
And I can't describe,
But there's something about the way you look tonight,
Takes my breath away.
The way you look tonight.

With that smile you pull the deepest secrets from my heart.
In all honesty, I'm speechless and I don't know where to start.

Refrain

The way you look tonight…

Sometimes When We Touch

Words by Dan Hill
Music by Barry Mann

recorded by Dan Hill

You ask me if I love you,
And I choke on my reply.
I'd rather hurt you honestly
Than mislead you with a lie.
And who am I to judge you
On what you say or do?
I'm only just beginning
To see the real you.

Refrain:
And sometimes when we touch,
The honesty's too much,
And I have to close my eyes and hide.
I wanna hold you till I die,
Till we both break down and cry,
I wanna hold you
Till the fear in me subsides.

Romance and all its strategy
Leaves me battling with my pride
But through the insecurity
Some tenderness survives.
I'm just another writer
Still trapped within my truths;
A hesitant prize-fighter
Still trapped within my youth.

At times I'd like to break you
And drive you to your knees.
At times I'd like to break through
And hold you endlessly.

At times I understand you,
And I know how hard you've tried,
I've watched while love commands you,
And I've watched love pass you by.
At times I think we're drifters,
Still searching for a friend,
A brother or a sister.
But then the passion flares again.

Refrain

Sorry Seems to Be the Hardest Word

Words and Music by Elton John and Bernie Taupin

recorded by Elton John

What have I got to do to make you love me?
What have I got to do to make you care?
What do I do when lightning strikes me
And I wake to find that you're not there?
What do I do to make you want me?
What have I gotta do to be heard?
What do I say when it's all over?
Sorry seems to be the hardest word.

Refrain:
It's sad, (It's so sad.)
It's so sad.
It's a sad, sad situation,
And it's getting more and more absurd.
It's sad, (It's so sad.)
It's so sad.
Why can't we talk it over?
Always seems to me
That sorry seems to be the hardest word.

Refrain

What do I do to make you love me?
What have I gotta do to be heard?
What do I do when lightning strikes me?
What have I got to do,
What have I got to do?
Sorry seems to be the hardest word.

Southern Cross

Words and Music by Stephen Stills, Richard Curtis and Michael Curtis

recorded by Crosby, Stills & Nash

Got out of town on a boat
Gon' to southern islands.
Sailing a reach before a following sea.
She was making for the trades
On the outside
And the downhill run to Papeete.

Off the wind on this heading,
Lie the Marquesas.
We got eighty feet of waterline,
Nicely makin' way.
In a noisy bar in Avalon,
I tried to call you.
But on the midnight watch I realized
Why twice you ran away.

Refrain:
Think about how many times I have fallen.
Spirits are usin' me; larger voices callin'.
What heaven brought you and me
Cannot be forgotten.
I have been around the world,
Lookin' for that woman-girl
Who knows love can endure.
And you know it will.

When you see the Southern Cross
For the first time,
You understand now why you came this way.
'Cause the truth you might be runnin' from is
   so small.
But it's big as the promise,
The promise of a comin' day.

So I'm sailing tomorrow.
My dreams are a-dying.
And my love is an anchor tied to you,
Tied with a silver chain.
I have my ship,
And all her flags are a-flying.
She is all that I have left,
And music is her name.

Refrain

So we cheated and we lied and we tested.
And we never failed to fail.
It was the easiest thing to do.
You will survive being bested.
Somebody fine will come along,
Make me forget about loving you
In the Southern Cross.

Sunshine on My Shoulders

Words by John Denver
Music by John Denver, Mike Taylor and Dick Kniss

recorded by John Denver

Refrain:
Sunshine on my shoulders makes me happy,
Sunshine in my eyes can make me cry.
Sunshine on the water looks so lovely,
Sunshine almost always makes me high.

If I had a day that I could give you,
I'd give to you a day just like today.
If I had a song that I could sing for you,
I'd sing a song to make you feel this way.

Refrain

If I had a tale that I could tell you,
I'd tell a tale sure to make you smile.
If I had a wish that I could wish for you,
I'd make a wish for sunshine all the while.

Refrain

Sunshine almost always makes me high...

Superman (It's Not Easy)

Words and Music by John Ondrasik

recorded by Five For Fighting

I can't stand to fly.
I'm not that naïve.
I'm just out to find
The better part of me.

I'm more than a bird.
I'm more than a plane.
I'm more than some pretty face
   beside a train.
And it's not easy to be me.

I wish that I could cry,
Fall upon my knees,
Find a way to lie
'Bout a home I'll never see.

It may sound absurd,
But don't be naïve.
Even heroes have the right to bleed.

I may be disturbed,
But won't you concede
Even heroes have the right to dream?
And it's not easy to be me.

Up, up and away, away from me.
Well it's alright, you can all sleep
   sound tonight.
I'm not crazy or anything.

I can't stand to fly.
I'm not that naïve.
Men weren't meant to ride
With clouds between their knees.

I'm only a man
In a silly red sheet,
Digging for kryptonite on this
   one-way street.

Only a man
In a silly red sheet
Looking for special things inside of me,

Inside of me, inside of me.
Yeah, inside of me, inside of me.

I'm only a man
In a funny red sheet.
I'm only a man looking for a dream.

I'm only a man
In a funny red sheet
And it's not easy, ooh, ooh, ooh.
It's not easy to be me.

Sweet Baby James

Words and Music by James Taylor

recorded by James Taylor

There is a young cowboy, he lives on the range,
His horse and his cattle are his only companions.
He works in the saddle and sleeps in the canyons,
Waiting for summer, his pastures to change.
And as the moon rises he sits by his fire,
Thinking about women and glasses of beer,
And closing his eyes as the doggies retire.
He sings out a song which is soft but it's clear,
As if maybe someone could hear.
He says

Refrain:
Goodnight you moonlight ladies,
Rockabye Sweet Baby James.
Deep greens and blues are the colors I choose,
Won't you let me go down in my dreams,
And rockabye Sweet Baby James.

The first of December was covered with snow
So was the turnpike from Stockbridge to Boston
The Berkshires seemed dream-like on account of that frosting
With ten miles behind me and ten thousand more to go.

There's a song that they sing when they take to the highway,
A song that they sing when they take to the sea,
A song that they sing of their home in the sky,
Maybe you can believe it if it helps you to sleep,
But singing works just fine for me.

Refrain

Take Me Home, Country Roads

Words and Music by John Denver, Bill Danoff and Taffy Nivert

recorded by John Denver

Almost heaven, West Virginia,
Blue Ridge Mountains, Shenandoah River.
Life is old there, older than the trees,
Younger than the mountains growin' like a breeze.

Refrain:
Country roads, take me home
To the place I belong:
West Virginia, mountain momma,
Take me home, country roads.

All memories gather 'round her,
Miner's lady, stranger to blue water.
Dark and dusty, painted on the sky,
Misty taste of moonshine, teardrop in my eye.

Refrain

I hear her voice, in the mornin' hour she calls me,
The radio reminds me of my home far away,
And drivin' down the road I get a feelin'
That I should have been home yesterday,
Yesterday.

Refrain

Country roads, take me home.

Take My Breath Away (Love Theme)

Words and Music by Giorgio Moroder and Tom Whitlock

from the Paramount Picture *Top Gun*
recorded by Berlin

Watching ev'ry motion
In my foolish lover's game;
On this endless ocean,
Fin'lly lovers know no shame.
Turning and returning
To some secret place inside;
Watching in slow motion
As you turn around and say,
"Take my breath away.
Take my breath away."

Watching, I keep waiting,
Still anticipating love,
Never hesitating
To become the fated ones.
Turning and returning
To some secret place to hide;
Watching in slow motion
As you turn my way and say,
"Take my breath away."

Through the hourglass I saw you.
In time, you slipped away.
When the mirror crashed, I called you
And turned to hear you say,
"If only for today
I am unafraid.
Take my breath away.
Take my breath away."

Watching ev'ry motion
In my foolish lover's game;
Haunted by the notion
Somewhere there's a love in flames.
Turning and returning
To some secret place inside;
Watching in slow motion
As you turn to me and say,
"Take my breath away.
My love, take my breath away.
My love, take my breath away."

Tapestry

Words and Music by Carole King

recorded by Carole King

My life has been a tapestry of rich and royal hue,
An everlasting vision of the ever-changing view.
A wondrous woven magic in bits of blue and gold
A tapestry to feel and see, impossible to hold.

Once, amid the soft, silver sadness in the sky,
There came a man of fortune, a drifter passing by.
He wore a torn and tattered cloth around his leathered hide,
And a coat of many colors, yellow, green on either side.

He moved with some uncertainty, as if he didn't know
Just what he was there for, or where he ought to go.
Once he reached for something golden, hanging from a tree,
And his hand came down empty.

Soon within my tapestry, along the rutted road,
He sat down on a river rock and turned into a toad.
It seemed that he had fallen into someone's wicked spell,
And I wept to see him suffer, though I didn't know him well.

As I watched in sorrow, there suddenly appeared
A figure, gray and ghostly, beneath a flowing beard.
In times of deepest darkness, I've seen him dressed in black.
Now my tapestry's unraveling; he's come to take me back.
He's come to take me back.

Teach Your Children

Words and Music by Graham Nash

recorded by Crosby, Stills, Nash & Young

You who are on the road
Must have a code
That you can live by,
And so
Become yourself,
Because the past
Is just a goodbye.

Teach your children well;
Their father's hell
Did slowly go by.
And feed
Them on your dreams,
The one they pick,
The one you'll know by.

Refrain:
Don't you ever ask them why;
If they told you, you would cry,
So just look at them and sigh
And know they love you.

(Can you hear and do you care?
Do you see,
You must be free,
To teach your children?
You'll believe they'll make a world
That we can live in.)

Teach your parents well;
Their children's hell
Will slowly go by.
And feed them on your dreams,
The one they pick,
The one you'll know by.

Refrain

Tears in Heaven

Words and Music by Eric Clapton and Will Jennings

recorded by Eric Clapton

Would you know my name
If I saw you in heaven?
Would it be the same
If I saw you in heaven?
I must be strong and carry on,
'Cause I know I don't belong
Here in heaven.

Would you hold my hand
If I saw you in heaven?
Would you help me stand
If I saw you in heaven?
I'll find my way through night and day,
'Cause I know I just can't stay
Here in heaven.

Time can bring you down,
Time can bend your knees.
Time can break your heart,
Have you beggin' please, beggin' please.

Beyond the door
There's peace, I'm sure,
And I know there'll be no more
Tears in heaven.

Repeat Verse 1

There You'll Be

Words and Music by Diane Warren

from Touchstone Pictures'/Jerry Bruckheimer Films' *Pearl Harbor*
recorded by Faith Hill

When I think back on these times
And the dreams we left behind,
I'll be glad, 'cause I was blessed to get,
To have you in my life.
When I think back on these days
I'll look and see your face.
You were right there for me.

In my dreams I'll always see
You soar above the sky.
In my heart there'll always be
A place for you, for all my life.
I'll keep a part of you with me,
And ev'rywhere I am, there you'll be,
And ev'rywhere I am, there you'll be.

Well, you showed me how it feels
To feel the sky within my reach,
And I always will remember
All the strength you gave to me.
Your love made me make it through;
Oh, I owe so much to you.
You were right there for me.

In my dreams I'll always see
You soar above the sky.
In my heart there'll always be
A place for you, for all my life.
I'll keep a part of you with me,
And ev'rywhere I am, there you'll be.

'Cause I always saw in you my light, my
   strength,
And I wanna thank you now for all the ways
You were right there for me.
You were right there for me, for always.

In my dreams I'll always see
You soar above the sky.
In my heart there'll always be
A place for you, for all my life.
I'll keep a part of you with me,
And ev'rywhere I am, there you'll be,
And ev'rywhere I am, there you'll be.
There you'll be.

THE LYRIC LIBRARY

These Are the Best Times

Words and Music by Shane Tatum

from Walt Disney Productions' *Superdad*

These are the best times,
The moments we can't let slip away.
Life's little game we play,
Living from day to day.

But once in a lifetime,
A minute like this is our to share.
Remember these moments well,
For moments like these are rare…

As dreams and golden rainbows,
Soft as night when summer wind blows by
Together we laugh and cry,
Together we'll learn to fly.

Come take my hand,
Together we'll cross the timeless sands,
Chasing the endless sun
Living our lives as one.

This Masquerade

Words and Music by Leon Russell

recorded by George Benson, The Carpenters

Are we really happy here with this lonely game we play,
Looking for words to say?
Searching but not finding understanding in any way,
We're lost in a masquerade.

Both afraid to say we're just to far away
From being close together from the start.
We tried to talk it over, but the words got in the way.
We're lost inside this lonely game we play.

Thoughts of leaving disappear everytime I see your eyes.
No matter how hard I try
To understand the reasons that we carry on this way,
We're lost in this masquerade.

This One's for You

Lyric by Marty Panzer
Music by Barry Manilow

recorded by Barry Manilow

This one'll never sell, they'll never understand.
I don't even sing it well, I try but I just can't.
But I sing it ev'ry night, and I fight to keep it in,
'Cause this one's for you, this one's for you.

I've done a hundred songs, from fantasies to lies,
But this one's so real for me that I'm that one who cries.
But I sing it ev'ry night, and I fight to hide the tears,
'Cause this one's for you, this one's for you.

This one's for you, wherever you are,
To say that nothing's been the same
Since we've been apart.
This one's for all the love we once knew,
Like ev'rything else I have, this one's for you.

I've got it all, it seems, for all it means to me,
But I sing of things I miss and things that used to be.
And I wonder every night if you might just miss me too,
And I sing for you, I sing for you.

This one's for you, wherever I go,
To say the things I should have said,
Things that you should know.
This one's to say that all I can do
Is hope that you will hear me sing
'Cause this one's for you.

This one's for you, wherever you are,
To say that nothing's been the same
Since we've been apart.

Three Times a Lady

Words and Music by Lionel Richie

recorded by The Commodores

Thanks for the times that you've given me,
The memories are all in my mind.
And now that we've come to the end of our rainbow,
There's something I must say out loud:

Refrain:
You're once, twice, three times a lady,
And I love you,
Yes, your once, twice, three times a lady,
And I love you,
I love you.

When we are together, the moments I cherish,
With every beat of my heart,
To touch you, to hold you, to feel you, to need you,
There's nothing to keep us apart.

Refrain

Time After Time

Words and Music by Cyndi Lauper and Rob Hyman

recorded by Cyndi Lauper, Inoj

Lyin' in my bed I hear the clock tick
and think of you,
Caught up in circles confusion is
nothing new.
Flash back
Warm nights,
Almost left behind.
Suitcase of memories
Time after time.

Sometimes you picture me
I'm walking too far ahead.
You're calling to me,
Can't hear what you've said.
Then you say go slow,
I fall behind.
The second hand unwinds.

Refrain:
If you're lost you can look
And you will find me
Time after time.
If you fall I will catch you
I'll be waiting
Time after time.

Repeat Refrain

After my picture fades
And darkness returned to gray.
Watching through windows,
You're wondering if I'm O.K.
Secrets stolen
From deep inside.
The drum beats out of time.

Refrain

Time after time.

Time in a Bottle

Words and Music by Jim Croce

recorded by Jim Croce

If I could save time in a bottle,
The first thing that I'd like to do,
Is to save every day 'til eternity passes away,
Just to spend them with you.

If I could make days last forever,
If words could make wishes come true,
I'd save every day like a treasure and then
I would spend them with you.

Refrain:
But there never seems to be enough time
To do the things you want to do
Once you find them.
I've looked round enough to know
That you're the one I want to go through time with.

If I had a box just for wishes,
And dreams that had never come true,
The box would be empty,
Except for the memory
Of how they were answered by you.

Refrain

To All the Girls I've Loved Before

Lyric by Hal David
Music by Albert Hammond

recorded by Julio Iglesias & Willie Nelson

To all the girls I've loved before,
Who traveled in and out my door;
I'm glad they came along,
I dedicate this song
To all the girls I've loved before.

To all the girls I once caressed
And may I say I've held the best;
For helping me to grow,
I owe a lot, I know,
To all the girls I've loved before.

Refrain:
The winds of change are always blowing
And ev'ry time I tried to stay,
The winds of change continued blowing
And they just carried me away.

To all the girls who shared my life,
Who now are someone else's wife;
I'm glad they came along,
I dedicate this song
To all the girls I've loved before.

To all the girls who cared for me,
Who filled my nights with ecstasy;
They live within my heart,
I'll always be a part
Of all the girls I've loved before.

Refrain

To all the girls we've loved before,
Who traveled in and out our door;
We're glad they came along,
We dedicate this song
To all the girls we've loved before.

(I've Had) The Time of My Life

Words and Music by Franke Previte, John DeNicola and Donald Markowitz

from the film *Dirty Dancing*
recorded by Bill Medley & Jennifer Warnes

Male:
Now I've had the time of my life.
No, I never felt like this before.
Yes, I swear it's the truth,
And I owe it all to you.

Female:
'Cause I've had the time of my life,
And I owe it all to you.

Male:
I've been waiting for so long;
Now I've fin'lly found someone
To stand by me.

Female:
We saw the writing on the wall
As we felt this magical fantasy.

Both:
Now with passion in our eyes,
There's no way we could disguise it secretly.
So we take each other's hand,
'Cause we seem to understand the urgency.

Male:
Just remember,

Female:
You're the one thing

Male:
I can't get enough of.

Female:
So I'll tell you something:

Both:
This could be love because

Refrain:
I've had the time of my life.
No, I never felt this way before.
Yes, I swear it's the truth,
And I owe it all to you.

Male:
Hey, baby.

Female:
With my body and soul,
I want you more than you'll ever know.

Male:
So we'll just let it go;
Don't be afraid to lose control.

Female:
Yes, I know what's on your mind
When you say, "Stay with me tonight."

Male:
Stay with me. Just remember,
You're the one thing

Female:
I can't get enough of.

Male:
So I'll tell you something:

Both:
This could be love because

Refrain

'Cause I had the time of my life.
And I've searched through ev'ry open door
Till I've found the truth,
And I owe it all to you.

To Be with You

Words and Music by Eric Martin and David Grahame

recorded by Mr. Big

Hold on, little girl,
Show me what he's done to you.
Stand up, little girl,
A broken heart can't be that bad.
When it's through, it's through.
Fate will twist the both of you.
So come on, baby, come on over,
Let me be the one to show you.

Refrain:
I'm the one who wants to be with you.
Deep inside I hope you feel it too.
(Feel it too.)
Waited on a line of greens and blues,
Just to be the next to be with you.

Build up your confidence,
So you can be on top for once.
Wake up, who cares about
Little boys that talk too much.
I seen it all go down.
Your game of love was all rained out.
So come on, baby, come on over,
Let me be the one to hold you.

Refrain

Why be alone, when we can be together,
  baby?
You can make my life worthwhile.
I can make you start to smile.

When it's through, it's through.
Fate will twist the both of you.
So come on, baby, come on over,
Let me be the one to show you.

Refrain

Just to be the next to be with you.

Touch Me in the Morning

Words and Music by Ronald Miller and Michael Masser

recorded by Diana Ross

Touch me in the morning,
Then just walk away.
We don't have tomorrow,
But we had yesterday.

(Hey!) Wasn't it me who said that
Nothing good's gonna last forever?
And wasn't it me who said
Let's just be glad for the time together?
Must've been hard to tell me
That you've given all you had to give.
I can understand your feeling that way.
Ev'rybody's got their life to live.

Well, I can say good-bye
In the cold morning light.
But I can't watch love die
In the warmth of the night.
If I've got to be strong,
Don't you know I
Need to have tonight when you're gone?
Till you go I need to lie here and
   think about
The last time that you'll

Touch me in the morning
Then just close the door.
Leave me as you found me,
Empty like before.

(Hey!) Wasn't it yesterday
We used to laugh at the wind behind us?
Didn't we run away and hope
That time wouldn't try to find us?
Didn't we take each other
To a place where no one's ever been?
Yeah, I really need you near me tonight,
'Cause you'll never take me there again.
Let me watch you go
With the sun in my eyes.
We've seen how love can grow,
Now we'll see how it dies.

If I've got to be strong,
Don't you know I need
To have tonight when you're gone?
Till you go I need to hold you
Until the time your hands reach out and

Duet with Verse 1:
Mornings were blue and gold,
And we could feel one another living.
We walked with a dream to hold,
And we could take what the world
   was giving.
There's no tomorrow here,
There's only love and the time to chase it.
Yesterday's gone, my love,
There's only now and it's time to face it.

True Colors

Words and Music by Billy Steinberg and Tom Kelly

recorded by Cyndi Lauper, Phil Collins

You with the sad eyes,
Don't be discouraged.
Oh, I realize
It's hard to take courage.
In a world full of people
You can lose sight of it all,
And the darkness inside you
Makes you feel so small.
But I see

Refrain:
Your true colors, shinin' through.
I see your true colors,
And that's why I love you.
So don't be afraid to let them show.
Your true colors,
True colors are beautiful,
Like a rainbow.

Show me your smile then,
Don't be unhappy.
Can't remember when
I last saw you laughing.
If this world makes you crazy
And you're takin' all you can bear,
Just call me up
Because you know I'll be there.
And I'll see

Refrain

Such sad eyes.
Take courage now and realize
When this world makes you crazy
And you're takin' all you can bear,
Just call me up
Because you know I'll be there.
And I see

Your true colors, shinin' through.
I see your true colors,
And that's why I love you.
So don't be afraid to let them show.
Your true colors, true colors,
True colors are shinin' through.
I see your true colors,
And that's why I love you.
So don't be afraid, just let them show.
Your true colors, true colors,
True colors are beautiful,
Beautiful like a rainbow.
Show me your colors.
Show me your rainbow.

Two Hearts

Words and Music by Phil Collins and Lamont Dozier

recorded by Phil Collins

There was no reason to believe
She'd always be there.
But if you don't put faith in what you believe in,
It's getting nowhere.
'Cause it helps you never give up,
Don't look down, just look up.
'Cause she's always there behind you,
Just to remind you.

Two hearts living in just one mind.
You know we're two hearts living in just one mind.

Well, there's no easy way to, to understand it.
There's so much of my life in her,
And it's like I planned it.
And it teaches you to never let go.
There's so much love you'll never know.
She can reach you no matter how far,
Wherever you are.

Refrain:
Two hearts living in just one mind.
Beating together till the end of time.
You know we're two hearts living in just one mind,
Together forever till the end of time.

She knows there'll always be
A special place in my heart for her.
She knows, she knows, she knows,
Yeah, she knows, no matter how far apart we are,
She knows I'm always right there beside her.

Refrain

Until It's Time for You to Go

Words and Music by Buffy Sainte-Marie

recorded by Buffy Sainte-Marie, Elvis Presley

I'm not a dream, I'm not an angel, I'm a man;
You're not a queen, you're a woman, take my hand.
We'll make a space in the lives that we planned.
And here we'll stay until it's time for you to go.

Yes we're different, worlds apart, we're not the same.
We laughed and played at the start like in a game.
You could have stayed outside my heart but in you came.
And here you'll stay until it's time for you to go.

Don't ask why.
Don't ask how.
Don't ask forever.
Love me now!

This love of mine had no beginning, has no end;
I was an oak now I'm a willow now I can bend.
And tho' I'll never in my life see you again.
Still I'll stay until it's time for you to go.

Vision of Love

Words and Music by Mariah Carey and Ben Margulies

recorded by Mariah Carey

Treated me kind.
Sweet destiny
Carried me through desperation
To the one that was waiting for me.
It took so long,
Still I believed
Somehow the one that I needed
Would find me eventually.

Refrain:
I had a vision of love,
And it was all that you've given to me.

Prayed through the nights,
Felt so alone.
Suffered from alienation,
Carried the weight on my own.
Had to be strong,
So I believed,
And now I know I've succeeded
In finding the place I conceived.

Refrain Twice

I've realized a dream,
And I visualized
The love that came to be.
Feel so alive.
I'm so thankful that I've received
The answer that heaven has sent down
    to me.

You treated me kind,
Sweet destiny,
And I'll be eternally grateful,
Holding you so close to me.
Prayed through the nights
So faithfully,
Knowing the one that I needed
Would find me eventually.

Refrain

I had a vision of love
And it was all that you turned out to be.

The Way We Were

Words by Alan and Marilyn Bergman
Music by Marvin Hamlisch

from the Motion Picture *The Way We Were*
recorded by Barbra Streisand

Memories
Light the corners of my mind.
Misty water-color memories
Of the way we were.

Scattered pictures
Of the smiles we left behind,
Smiles we gave to one another
For the way we were.

Can it be that it was all so simple then,
Or has time rewritten every line?
If we had the chance to do it all again,
Tell me would we? Could we?

Memories
May be beautiful, and yet,
What's too painful to remember
We simply choose to forget.

So it's the laughter
We will remember,
Whenever we remember
The way we were,
The way we were.

We Just Disagree

Words and Music by Jim Krueger

recorded by Dave Mason, Billy Dean

Been away.
Haven't seen you in a while.
How've you been?
Have you changed your style?
And do you think that we're grown up different?
It don't seem the same.
Seems you've lost your feel for me.

Refrain:
So let's leave it alone
'Cause we can't see eye to eye.
There ain't no good guy.
There ain't no bad guy.
There's only you and me, and we just disagree.

Ooh. Oh, oh.
I'm going back to a place that's far away.
How 'bout you?
Have you got a place to stay?
Why should I care when I'm just tryin' to get along?
We were friends.
But now it's the end of our love song.

Refrain Twice

What a Wonderful World

Words and Music by George David Weiss and Bob Thiele

featured in the Motion Picture *Good Morning Vietnam*
recorded by Louis Armstrong

I see trees of green, red roses too,
I see them bloom for me and you,
And I think to myself
What a wonderful world.

I see skies of blue and clouds of white,
The bright blessed day, the dark sacred night,
And I think to myself
What a wonderful world.

The colors of the rainbow, so pretty in the sky
Are also on the faces of people goin' by.
I see friends shakin' hands, sayin', "How do you do?"
They're really sayin', "I love you."

I hear babies cry, I watch them grow.
They'll learn much more than I'll ever know.
And I think to myself,
What a wonderful world.
Yes, I think to myself
What a wonderful world.

When I Look into Your Eyes

Words and Music by Carl Snare and Bill Leverty

recorded by Firehouse

I see forever when I look in your eyes.
You're all I've ever wanted,
I always want you to be mine.
Let's make a promise till the end of time.
We'll always be together,
And our love will never die.

So, here we are face to face and heart
   to heart.
I want you to know we will never be apart.
Now I believe that wishes can come true,
'Cause I see my whole world.
   I see only you.

Refrain:
When I look into you eyes
I can see how much I love you
And it makes me realize.
When I look into your eyes
I see all my dreams come true.
When I look into your eyes.

I've looked for you all of my life.
Now that I've found you,
We will never say good-bye.
Can't stop this feelin'
And there's nothin' I can do
'Cause I see ev'rything when I look at you.

Refrain

Oh, when I look into your eyes
I can see how much I love you
And it makes me realize.
When I look into your eyes,
We will always be together,
And our love will never die.
When I look into your eyes
I see all my dreams come true.
When I look into your eyes,
When I look into your eyes.

When She Loved Me

Music and Lyrics by Randy Newman

from Walt Disney Pictures' *Toy Story 2—A Pixar Film*
recorded by Sarah McLachlan

When somebody loved me, everything was beautiful.
Every hour we spent together lives within my heart.
And when she was sad, I was there to dry her tears;
And when she was happy, so was I, when she loved me.

Through the summer and the fall,
We had each other that was all.
Just she and I together, like it was meant to be.
And when she was lonely, I was there to comfort her,
And I knew that she loved me.

So the years went by; I stayed the same.
But she began to drift away; I was left alone.
Still I waited for the day when she'd say,
"I will always love you."

Lonely and forgotten, never thought she'd look my way,
And she smiled at me and held me just like she used to,
Like she loved me when she loved me.
When somebody loved me, everything was beautiful.
Every hour we spent together lives within my heart,
When she loved me.

When You Believe (From The Prince Of Egypt)

Words and Music Composed by Stephen Schwartz
with Additional Music by Babyface

from the film *The Prince of Egypt*
recorded by Whitney Houston & Mariah Carey

Many nights we prayed,
With no proof anyone could hear.
In our hearts a hopeful song we barely
   understood.
Now we are not afraid,
Although we know there's much to fear.
We were moving mountains long before
   we knew we could.

Refrain:
There can be miracles,
When you believe.
Though hope is frail,
It's hard to kill.

Who knows what miracles
   you can achieve?
When you believe, somehow you will.
You will when you believe.

In this time of fear,
When prayer so often proves in vain,
Hope seems like the summer birds,
Too swiftly flown away.
Yet now I'm standing here,
My heart so full I can't explain,
Seeking faith and speaking words
I never thought I'd say:

There can be miracles,
When you believe.
Though hope is frail,
It's hard to kill.
Who knows what miracles you can achieve?
When you believe,
Somehow you will.
You will when you believe.

They don't always happen when you ask.
And it's easy to give in to your fear.
But when you're blinded by your pain,
Can't see your way clear through the rain,
A small but still resilient voice
Says help is very near.

Refrain

You will when you,
You will when you believe,
Just believe,
Just believe.
You will when you believe.

A Whole New World (Aladdin's Theme)

Music by Alan Menken
Lyrics by Tim Rice

from Walt Disney's *Aladdin*
recorded by Peabo Bryson & Regina Belle

I can show you the world,
Shining, shimmering, splendid.
Tell me princess, now when
Did you last let your heart decide?

I can open your eyes
Take you wonder by wonder
Over, sideways and under
On a magic carpet ride.

A whole new world
A new fantastic point of view.
No-one to tell us no
Or where to go
Or say we're only dreaming.

A whole new world
A dazzling place I never knew.
But when I'm way up here
It's crystal clear
That now I'm in a whole new world
  with you.
Unbelievable sights
Indescribable feeling.
Soaring, tumbling, free-wheeling
Through an endless diamond sky.

A whole new world
A hundred thousand things to begin.
I'm like a shooting star
I've come so far
I can't go back
I'm in a whole new world.

With new horizons to pursue.
I'll chase them anywhere.
There's time to spare.
Let me share
This whole new world with you.

A whole new world,
That's where we'll be.
A thrilling chase,
A wond'rous place
For you and me.

A Wink and a Smile

Music by Marc Shaiman
Lyrics by Ramsey McLean

featured in the TriStar Motion Picture *Sleepless in Seattle*
recorded by Harry Connick, Jr.

I remember the days of just keeping time,
Of hanging around in sleepy towns forever;
Back roads empty for miles.
Well, you can't have a dream and cut it to fit,
But when I saw you,
I knew we'd go together like a wink and a smile.

Leave your old jalopy by the railroad track.
We'll get a hip double dip tip-toppy two seat Cadillac.
So you can rev her up; and don't go slow,
It's only green lights and "All rights."
Lets go together with a wink and a smile.

Give me a wink and a smile.

We'd go together like a wink and a smile.
Now my heart hears music; such a simple song.
Sing it again; the notes never end.
This is where I belong.

Just the sound of your voice, the light in your eyes,
We're so far away from yesterday, together,
With a wink and a smile.
We go together like a wink and a smile.

With You I'm Born Again

Words by Carol Connors
Music by David Shire

recorded by Billy Preston & Syreeta

Man:
Come bring me your softness.
Comfort me through all this madness.
Woman, don't you know with you
I'm born again?

Woman:
Come give me your sweetness.
Now there's you, there is no weakness.
Lying safe within your arms
I'm born again.

Man*:
I was half, not whole,
In step with none.

Woman*:
Reaching through this world
In need of one.

Both:
Come show me your kindness.
In your arms I know I'll find this.

Man:
Woman, don't you know with you
I'm born again?

Woman:
Lying safe with you I'm born again.

Repeat song

*second time Both

Woman in Love

Words and Music by Barry Gibb and Robin Gibb

recorded by Barbra Streisand

Love is a moment in space,
When the dream is gone
It's a lonelier place.
I kiss the morning goodbye.
But down inside
You know we never know why.
The road is narrow and long
When eyes meet eyes
And the feeling is strong.
I turn away from the wall.
I stumble and fall,
But I give you it all.

Refrain:
I am a woman in love
And I'd do anything
To get you into my world
And hold you within.
It's a right I defend
Over and over again.

With you eternally mine,
In love there is
No measure of time.
We planned it all at the start,
That you and I
Live in each other's hearts.
We may be oceans away
You feel my love
I hear what you say.
The truth is ever a lie.
I stumble and fall,
But I give you it all.

Refrain

I am a woman in love
And I'm talkin' to you.
I know how you feel,
What a woman can do.
It's a right I defend
Over and over again

Refrain

Yesterday Once More

Words and Music by John Bettis and Richard Carpenter

recorded by The Carpenters

When I was young I'd listen to the radio
Waitin' for my favorite songs
When they played I'd sing along; it made me smile.
Those were such happy times and not so long ago,
How I wondered where they'd gone.
But they're back again just like a long lost friend,
All the songs I love so well.

Refrain:
Every sha-la-la-la, every wo, wo, wo still shines.
Every shinga-ling-a-ling that they're startin' to sing so fine.

When they get to the part where he's breaking her heart
It can really make me cry just like before.
It's yesterday once more.
(Shoobie do lang lang.)

Lookin' back on how it was in years gone by
And the good times that I had,
Makes today seem rather sad, so much has changed.
It was songs of love that I would sing to then.
And I'd memorize each word.
Those old melodies still sound so good to me,
As they melt the years away.

Refrain

All my best memories come back clearly to me,
Some can even make me cry just like before.

Repeat Refrain and Fade

You and Me Against the World

Words and Music by Paul Williams and Ken Ascher

recorded by Helen Reddy

You and me against the world.
Sometimes it feels like you and me against the world.
When all others turn their back and walk away,
You can count on me to stay.
Remember when the circus came to town,
And you were frightened by the clown?
Wasn't it nice to be around someone that you knew,
Someone who was big and strong,
And lookin' out for you and me against the world.

And for all the times we've cried,
I always felt the odds were on our side.
And when one of us is gone,
And one is left alone to carry on,
Well, then remembering will have to do.
Our memories alone will get us through.
Think about the days of me and you,
Of you and me against the world.

Life can be a circus.
They under pay and over work us,
And though we seldom get our due,
When each day is through,
I bring my tired body home,
And look around for me and you against the world.
Sometimes it feels like you and me against the world.
And for all the times we've cried,
I always felt that God was on our side.

And when one of us is gone,
And one is left alone to carry on,
Well, then remembering will have to do.
Our memories alone will get us through.
Think about the days of me and you,
Of you and me against the world.

You Decorated My Life

Words and Music by Debbie Hupp and Bob Morrison

recorded by Kenny Rogers

All my life was a paper,
Once plain, pure, and white,
Till you moved with your pen,
Changin' moods now and then
Till the balance was right.
Then you added some music,
Ev'ry note was in place;
And anybody could see all the changes in me
By the look on my face.

Refrain:
And you decorated my life,
Created a world where dreams are a part.
And you decorated my life
By paintin' your love all over my heart.
You decorated my life.

Like a rhyme with no reason
In an unfinished song,
There was no harmony,
Life meant nothin' to me
Until you came along.
And you brought out the colors,
What a gentle surprise;
Now I'm able to see all the things life can be,
Shinin' soft in your eyes.

Refrain

You Sang to Me

Words and Music by Cory Rooney and Marc Anthony

recorded by Marc Anthony

I just wanted you to comfort me
When I called you late last night.
You see, I was falling into love,
Yes, I was crashing into love.
Oh, of all the words you said to me
About life, the truth, and being free, yeah,
You sang to me, oh, how you sang to me.

Girl, I live for how you make me feel,
So I question all this being real,
'Cause I'm not afraid to love;
For the first time I'm not afraid of love.
Oh, this day seems made for you and me
And you showed me what life needs to be.
Yeah, you sang to me, oh, you sang to me.

Refrain:
All the while you were in front of me
  I never realized.
I just can't believe I didn't see it
  in your eyes.
I didn't see it, I can't believe it.
Oh, but I feel it when you sing to me.
How I long to hear you sing beneath the
  clear blue skies,
And I promise you this time I'll see it
  in your eyes.
I didn't see it, I can't believe it,
Oh, but I feel it when you sing to me.

Just to think you live inside of me.
I had no idea how this could be.
Now I'm crazy for your love.
Can't believe I'm crazy for your love.
The words you said just sang to me
And you showed me where I wanna be.
You sang to me, oh, you sang to me.

Refrain Twice

You're in My Heart

Words and Music by Rod Stewart

recorded by Rod Stewart

I didn't know what day it was
When you walked into the room.
I said hello. I noticed
You said good-bye too soon.

Breezin' through the clientele,
Spinning yarns that were so lyrical.
I really must confess right here,
The attraction was purely physical.

I took all those habits of yours
That in the beginning were hard to accept.
Your fashion sense, Beardsly prints,
I put down to experience.

The big-bosomed lady with the
   Dutch accent
Who tried to change my point of view.
Her ad-libbed lines were well rehearsed,
But my heart cried out for you.

Refrain:
You're in my heart. You're in my soul.
You'll be my breath should I grow old.
You are my lover, you're my best friend.
You're in my soul.

My love for you is immeasurable,
My respect for you immense.
You're ageless, timeless, lace and fineness.
You're beauty and elegance.

You're a rhapsody, a comedy.
You're a symphony and a play.
You're ev'ry love song ever written,
But honey, what do you see in me?

Refrain

You're an essay in glamor.
Please pardon the grammar,
But you're ev'ry schoolboy's dream.
You're Celtic united, but baby I've decided
You're the best team I've ever seen.

And there have been many affairs
And many times I've thought to leave.
But I bite my lip and turn around,
'Cause you're the warmest thing I've ever
   found.

Refrain

You're the Inspiration

Words and Music by Peter Cetera and David Foster

recorded by Chicago

You know our love was meant to be
The kind of love that lasts forever.
And I want you here with me
From tonight until the end of time.
You should know everywhere I go;
Always on my mind, in my heart,
In my soul, baby.

Refrain:
You're the meaning of my life,
You're the inspiration.
You bring feeling to my life,
You're the inspiration.

Wanna have you near me,
I wanna have you hear me saying
No one needs you more than I need you.
(No one needs you more than I.)

And I know (yes, I know)
That it's plain to see;
We're so in love when we're together.
Now I know (now I know)
That I need you here with me
From tonight to the end of time.
You should know everywhere I go;
Always on my mind, you're in my heart,
In my soul.

Refrain

Wanna have you near me,
I wanna have you hear me say yeah,
No one needs you more than I need you.
You're the meaning of my life,
You're the inspiration.
You bring feeling to my life,
You're the inspiration.

When you love somebody:
(Till the end of time;)
When you love somebody
(Always on my mind.)
No one needs you more than I.

You're Where I Belong

Words and Music by Diane Warren

from the Columbia Pictures film *Stuart Little*™
recorded by Trisha Yearwood

I am home now, home now.
I've been waiting for forever to find you,
    to find you.
I'm not alone now, alone now,
'Cause you've taken in my heart from
    the cold.
All I know is ev'ry time I look into
    your eyes,
I'm home, I know.

Refrain:
You're where I belong.
I belong with you.
You're where I belong,
And I know it's the truth.
You're part of my heart.
There's nothing I can do.
Oh, you're the one who keeps me warm.
My baby, you're where I belong.

You're my first taste, my first taste
Of the sweetest feeling I've ever known,
    that I've known.
You're my safe place, my safe place,
From a world that can be so cruel
    and cold.
You're my harbor, you're my shelter,
    you're that welcome smile
That lets me know I'm home.

Refrain

You're the one I come too, yeah,
To keep me from the cold.
You're where I belong.
I belong with you.
You're where I belong,
And I know it's the truth.
You're part of my heart.
There's nothin' I can do.
Oh, you're the one who keeps me warm.
My baby, you're where I belong.

(You're where I belong.
    You're my only home.)
You're where I belong.
(You're where I belong.
You're where I belong.
    You're my only home.)
You're where I belong.
(You're where I belong.
You're where I belong.
    You're my only home.)
You're where I belong.
I am home now, home now.

You've Got a Friend

Words and Music by Carole King

recorded by James Taylor, Carole King

When you're down and troubled,
And you need some loving care;
(or: And you need a helping hand;)
And nothin' is goin' right
Close your eyes and think of me,
And soon I will be there:
To brighten up even your darkest night.

You just call out my name,
And you know wherever I am
I'll come runnin' to see you again.
Winter, spring, summer or fall,
All you have to do is call,
And I'll be there.
You've got a friend.

If the sky above you
Grows dark and full of clouds;
And that old north wind begins to blow
Keep your head together,
And call my name out loud;
Soon you'll hear me knockin' at your door.

You just call out my name,
And you know wherever I am
I'll come runnin' to see you again.
Winter, spring, summer or fall,
All you have to do is call,
And I'll be there, yes, I will.

Now ain't it good to know that you've
   got a friend,
When people can be so cold.
They'll hurt you,
Yes, and desert you,
And take your soul if you let them.
Oh, but don't you let them.

You just call out my name,
And you know wherever I am
I'll come runnin' to see you a gain.
Winter, spring, summer or fall,
All you have to do is call,
And I'll be there, yes, I will.

You've got a friend.
You've got a friend.
Ain't it good to know
You've got a friend...

You've Got a Friend in Me

Music and Lyrics by Randy Newman

from Walt Disney's *Toy Story*
from Walt Disney Pictures' *Toy Story 2—A Pixar Film*
recorded by Randy Newman and Lyle Lovett

You've got a friend in me.
You've got a friend in me.
When the road looks rough ahead,
And your miles and miles from your nice warm bed,
You just remember what your old pal said:
Son, you've got a friend in me.
Yeah, you've got a friend in me.

You've got a friend in me.
You've got a friend in me.
You got troubles, then I got 'em too.
There isn't anything I wouldn't do for you.
If we stick together we can see it through,
'Cause you've got a friend in me.
Yeah, you've got a friend in me.

Now, some other folks might be a little bit smarter than I am,
Bigger and stronger too.
Maybe. But none of them will ever love you the way I do,
Just me and you, boy.

And as the years go by,
Our friendship will never die.
You're gonna see it's our destiny.

You've got a friend in me.
You've got a friend in me.
You've got a friend in me.

Artist Index

Five For Fighting
169 Superman (It's Not Easy)

Roberta Flack
39 The Closer I Get to You
59 Feel Like Makin' Love
117 Killing Me Softly with His Song

Dan Fogelberg
156 Same Old Lang Syne

Foreigner
94 I Want to Know What Love Is

Marvin Gaye
84 How Sweet It Is
      (To Be Loved by You)
130 Mercy, Mercy Me (The Ecology)

Genesis
110 Invisible Touch

Boy George
44 The Crying Game

Barry Gibb
68 Guilty

Debbie Gibson
124 Lost in Your Eyes

Goo Goo Dolls
111 Iris

Amy Grant
137 The Next Time I Fall

Al Green
103 I'm Still in Love With You

Donny Hathaway
39 The Closer I Get to You

Heart
17 Alone

Dan Hill
34 Can't We Try
165 Sometimes When We Touch

Faith Hill
32 Breathe
176 There You'll Be

Jordan Hill
153 Remember Me This Way

The Hollies
11 The Air That I Breathe
73 He Ain't Heavy…He's My Brother

Whitney Houston
157 Saving All My Love for You
197 When You Believe (From The
      Prince Of Egypt)

Janis Ian
23 At Seventeen

Enrique Iglesias
77 Hero

Julio Iglesias
183 To All the Girls I've Loved Before

James Ingram
88 I Don't Have the Heart
116 Just Once

Inoj
181 Time After Time

Michael Jackson
28 Ben

Billy Joel
20 And So It Goes
79 Honesty
127 Lullabye (Goodnight, My Angel)
136 New York State of Mind
159 She's Always a Woman
160 She's Got a Way

Elton John
38 Circle of Life
164 Something About the
      Way You Look Tonight
166 Sorry Seems to Be the
      Hardest Word

Quincy Jones
116 Just Once

K-Ci & JoJo
14 All My Life

Nicole Kidman
139 One Day I'll Fly Away

Carole King
37 Child of Mine
114 It's Too Late
162 So Far Away
173 Tapestry
209 You've Got a Friend

Cyndi Lauper
181 Time After Time
188 True Colors

Brenda Lee
44 The Crying Game

John Lennon
108 Imagine

Lonestar
19 Amazed

Loverboy
74 Heaven in Your Eyes

Lyle Lovett
210 You've Got a Friend in Me

Melissa Manchester
49 Don't Cry Out Loud
131 Midnight Blue

Barry Manilow
43 Could It Be Magic
56 Even Now
86 I Am Your Child
97 I Write the Songs
123 Looks Like We Made It
129 Mandy
151 Ready to Take a Chance Again
      (Love Theme)
179 This One's for You

Marilyn Martin
158 Separate Lives

Dave Mason
193 We Just Disagree

Paul McCartney
53 Ebony and Ivory

Sarah McLachlan
8 Adia
21 Angel
95 I Will Remember You
196 When She Loved Me

Bill Medley
184 (I've Had) The Time of My Life

Bette Midler
63 From a Distance

Mike & The Mechanics
120 The Living Years

Mr. Big
186 To Be with You

Anne Murray
90 I Just Fall in Love Again

Willie Nelson
18 Always on My Mind
64 Georgia on My Mind
183 To All the Girls I've Loved Before

New Kids on the Block
99 I'll Be Loving You (Forever)

Randy Newman
210 You've Got a Friend in Me

Songwriter Index

More Collections from The Lyric Library

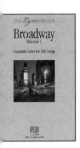

BROADWAY VOLUME I

An invaluable collection of lyrics to 200 top Broadway tunes, including: All at Once You Love Her • All I Ask of You • And All That Jazz • Any Dream Will Do • As Long As He Needs Me • At the End of the Day • Autumn in New York • Bali Ha'i • Bewitched • Cabaret • Castle on a Cloud • Climb Ev'ry Mountain • Comedy Tonight • Don't Rain on My Parade • Everything's Coming up Roses • Hello, Dolly! • I Could Have Danced All Night • I Dreamed a Dream • I Remember It Well • If I Were a Bell • It's the Hard-Knock Life • Let Me Entertain You • Mame • My Funny Valentine • Oklahoma • Seasons of Love • September Song • Seventy Six Trombones • Shall We Dance? • Springtime for Hitler • Summer Nights • Tomorrow • Try to Remember • Unexpected Song • What I Did for Love • With One Look • You'll Never Walk ne • (I Wonder Why?) You're Just in Love • and more.

_____00240201 ....$14.95

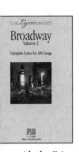

BROADWAY VOLUME II

200 more favorite Broadway lyrics (with no duplication from Volume I): Ain't Misbehavin' • All of You • Another Op'nin', Another Show • As If We Never Said Goodbye • Beauty School Dropout • The Best of Times • Bring Him Home • Brotherhood of Man • Camelot • Close Every Door • Consider Yourself • Do-Re-Mi • Edelweiss • Getting to Know You • Have You Met Miss Jones? • I Loved You Once in Silence • I'm Flying • If Ever I Would Leave You • The Impossible Dream (The Quest) • It Only Takes a Moment • The Lady Is a Tramp • The Last Night of the World • A Little More Mascara • Lost in the Stars • Love Changes Everything • Me and My Girl • Memory • My Heart Belongs to Daddy • On a Clear Day (You Can See Forever) • On My Own • People • Satin Doll • The Sound of Music • Sun and Moon • The rey with the Fringe on Top • Unusual Way (In a Very Unusual Way) • We Kiss in a Shadow • We Need a Little istmas • Who Will Buy? • Wishing You Were Somehow Here Again • Younger Than Springtime • and more.

_____00240205 ....$14.95

CHRISTMAS

200 lyrics to the most loved Christmas songs of all time, including: Angels We Have Heard on High • Auld Lang Syne • Away in a Manger • Baby, It's Cold Outside • The Chipmunk Song • The Christmas Shoes • The Christmas Song (Chestnuts Roasting on an Open Fire) • Christmas Time Is Here • Do They Know It's Christmas? • Do You Hear What I Hear • Feliz Navidad • The First Noel • Frosty the Snow Man • The Gift • God Rest Ye Merry, Gentlemen • Goin' on a Sleighride • Grandma Got Run over by a Reindeer • Happy Xmas (War Is Over) • He Is Born, the Holy Child (Il Est Ne, Le Divin Enfant) • The Holly and the Ivy • A Holly Jolly Christmas • (There's No Place Like) Home for the Holidays • I Heard the Bells on Christmas Day • I Wonder As I Wander • I'll Be Home for Christmas • I've Got My Love to ep Me Warm • In the Bleak Midwinter • It Came upon the Midnight Clear • It's Beginning to Look like Christmas t's Just Another New Year's Eve • Jingle Bells • Joy to the World • Mary, Did You Know? • Merry Christmas, Darling he Most Wonderful Time of the Year • My Favorite Things • Rudolph the Red-Nosed Reindeer • Silent Night • er Bells • The Twelve Days of Christmas • What Child Is This? • What Made the Baby Cry? • Wonderful istmastime • and more.

_____00240206 ....$14.95

See our website for a complete contents list for each volume:
www.halleonard.com

FOR MORE INFORMATION, SEE YOUR LOCAL MUSIC DEALER,
OR WRITE TO:

HAL•LEONARD® CORPORATION

7777 W. BLUEMOUND RD. P.O. BOX 13819 MILWAUKEE, WI 53213

Prices, contents and availability subject to change without notice.

More Collections from The Lyric Library

CLASSIC ROCK

Lyrics to 200 essential rock classics songs, including: All Day and All of the Night • All Right Now • Angie • Another One Bites the Dust • Back in the U.S.S.R. • Ballroom Blitz • Barracuda • Beast of Burden • Bell Bottom Blues • Brain Damage • Brass in Pocket • Breakdown • Breathe • Bus Stop • California Girls • Carry on Wayward Son • Centerfold • Changes • Cocaine • Cold As Ice • Come Sail Away • Come Together • Crazy Little Thing Called Love • Crazy on You • Don't Do Me like That • Don't Fear the Reaper • Don't Let the Sun Go down on Me • Don't Stand So Close to Me • Dreamer • Drive My Car • Dust in the Wind • 867-5309/Jenny • Emotional Rescue • Every Breath You Take • Every Little Thing She Does Is Magic • Eye in the Sky • Eye of the Tiger • Fame • Forever Young • Fortress Around Your Heart • Free Ride • Give a Little Bit • Gloria • Godzilla • Green-Eyed Lady • Heartache Tonight • Heroes • Hey Joe • Hot Blooded • I Fought the Law • I Shot the Sheriff • I Won't Back Down • Instant Karma • Invisible Touch • It's Only Rock 'N' Roll (But I like It) • It's Still Rock and Roll to Me • Layla • The Logical Song • Long Cool Woman (In a Black Dress) • Love Hurts • Maggie May • Me and Bobby McGee • Message in a Bottle • Mississippi Queen • Money • Money for Nothing • My Generation • New Kid in Town • Nights in White Satin • Paradise by the Dashboard Light • Piano Man • Rebel, Rebel • Refugee • Rhiannon • Roxanne • Shattered • Smoke on the Water • Sultans of Swing • Sweet Emotion • Walk This Way • We Gotta Get Out of This Place • We Will Rock You • Wouldn't It Be Nice • and many more!

_____00240183 ....$14.95

CONTEMPORARY CHRISTIAN

An amazing collection of 200 lyrics from some of the most prominent Contemporary Christian artists: Abba (Father) • After the Rain • Angels • Awesome God • Breathe on Me • Circle of Friends • Doubly Good to You • Down on My Knees • El Shaddai • Father's Eyes • Friends • Give It Away • Go Light Your World • God's Own Fool • Grand Canyon • The Great Adventure • The Great Divide • He Walked a Mile • Heaven and Earth • Heaven in the Real World • His Strength Is Perfect • Household of Faith • How Beautiful • I Surrender All • Jesus Freak • Joy in the Journey • Judas' Kiss • A Little More • Live Out Loud • Love Will Be Our Home • A Maze of Grace • The Message • My Utmost for His Highest • Oh Lord, You're Beautiful • People Need the Lord • Pray • Say the Name • Signs of Life • Speechless • Stand • Steady On • Via Dolorosa • The Warrior Is a Child • What Matters Most • Would I Know You • and more.

_____00240184 ....$14.95

COUNTRY

A great resource of lyrics to 200 of the best country songs of all time, including: Act Naturally • All My Ex's Live in Texas • All the Gold in California • Always on My Mind • Amazed • American Made • Angel of the Morning • Big Bad John • Blue • Blue Eyes Crying in the Rain • Boot Scootin' Boogie • Breathe • By the Time I Get to Phoenix • Could I Have This Dance • Crazy • Daddy's Hands • D-I-V-O-R-C-E • Down at the Twist and Shout • Elvira • Folsom Prison Blues • Friends in Low Places • The Gambler • Grandpa (Tell Me 'Bout the Good Old Days) • Harper Valley P.T.A. • He Thinks He'll Keep Her • Hey, Good Lookin' • I Fall to Pieces • I Hope You Dance • I Love a Rainy Night • I Saw the Light • I've Got a Tiger by the Tail • Islands in the Stream • Jambalaya (On the Bayou) • The Keeper of the Stars • King of the Road • Lucille • Make the World Go Away • Mammas Don't Let Your Babies Grow up to Be Cowboys • My Baby Thinks He's a Train • Okie from Muskogee • Ring of Fire • Rocky Top • Sixteen Tons • Stand by Me • There's a Tear in My Beer • Walkin' After Midnight • When You Say Nothing at All • Where the Stars and Stripes and the Eagle Fly • Where Were You (When the World Stopped Turning) • You Are My Sunshine • Your Cheatin' Heart • and more.

_____00240204 ....$14.95

See our website for a complete contents list for each volume:
www.halleonard.com

For More Information, See Your Local Music Dealer,
Or Write To:

HAL•LEONARD®
CORPORATION
7777 W. Bluemound Rd. P.O. Box 13819 Milwaukee, WI 53213

Prices, contents and availability subject to change without notice.

lore Collections from The Lyric Library

EARLY ROCK 'N' ROLL

Lyrics to 200 top songs that started the rock 'n' roll revolution, including: All I Have to Do Is Dream • All Shook Up • At the Hop • Baby Love • Barbara Ann • Be-Bop-A-Lula • Big Girls Don't Cry • Blue Suede Shoes • Bo Diddley • Book of Love • Calendar Girl • Chantilly Lace • Charlie Brown • Crying • Dancing in the Street • Do Wah Diddy Diddy • Don't Be Cruel (To a Heart That's True) • Earth Angel • Fun, Fun, Fun • Great Balls of Fire • He's a Rebel • Heatwave (Love Is like a Heatwave) • Hello Mary Lou • Hound Dog • I Walk the Line • It's My Party • Kansas City • The Loco-Motion • My Boyfriend's Back • My Guy • Oh, Pretty Woman • Peggy Sue • Rock and Roll Is Here to Stay • Sixteen Candles • Splish Splash • Stand by Me • Stupid Cupid • Surfin' U.S.A. • Teen Angel • A Teenager in Love • Twist and Shout • k like a Man • Where the Boys Are • Why Do Fools Fall in Love • Willie and the Hand Jive • and more.

____00240203 ....$14.95

LOVE SONGS

Lyrics to 200 of the most romantic songs ever written, including: All My Loving • Always in My Heart (Siempre En Mi Corazon) • And I Love Her • Anniversary Song • Beautiful in My Eyes • Call Me Irresponsible • Can You Feel the Love Tonight • Cheek to Cheek • (They Long to Be) Close to You • Could I Have This Dance • Dedicated to the One I Love • Don't Know Much • Dream a Little Dream of Me • Endless Love • Fields of Gold • For Once in My Life • Grow Old with Me • The Hawaiian Wedding Song (Ke Kali Nei Au) • Heart and Soul • Hello, Young Lovers • How Deep Is the Ocean (How High Is the Sky) • I Just Called to Say I Love You • I'll Be There • I've Got My Love to Keep Me Warm • Just the Way You Are • Longer • L-O-V-E • Love Will Keep Us Together • Misty • Moonlight in Vermont • More (Ti Guardero' Cuore) • My Funny Valentine • My Heart Will Go on (Love Theme from 'Titanic') • She • Speak Softly, Love (Love me) • Till • A Time for Us (Love Theme) • Unchained Melody • Up Where We Belong • We've Only Just Begun hat the World Needs Now Is Love • When I Fall in Love • Witchcraft • Wonderful Tonight • You Are the Sunshine ly Life • You're the Inspiration • You've Made Me So Very Happy • and more!

____00240186 ....$14.95

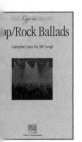

POP/ROCK BALLADS

Lyrics to 200 top tunes of the pop/rock era, including: Adia • After the Love Has Gone • Against All Odds (Take a Look at Me Now) • Always on My Mind • Amazed • And So It Goes • Baby What a Big Surprise • Ben • Breathe • Change the World • Come to My Window • Do You Know Where You're Going To? • Don't Cry Out Loud • Don't Fall in Love with a Dreamer • Don't Let Me Be Lonely Tonight • Easy • Feelings (?Dime?) • Fire and Rain • From a Distance • Georgia on My Mind • Hero • I Hope You Dance • Imagine • In the Air Tonight • Iris • Just My Imagination (Running Away with Me) • Killing Me Softly with His Song • Laughter in the Rain • Looks like We Made It • My Heart Will Go on (Love Theme from 'Titanic') • New York State of Mind • The Rainbow Connection • Rainy Days and days • Sailing • She's Always a Woman • Sing • Sunshine on My Shoulders • Take Me Home, Country Roads • rs in Heaven • There You'll Be • Time After Time • Vision of Love • The Way We Were • Woman in Love • You're Inspiration • You've Got a Friend • and more.

____00240187 ....$14.95

See our website for a complete contents list for each volume:
www.halleonard.com

FOR MORE INFORMATION, SEE YOUR LOCAL MUSIC DEALER,
OR WRITE TO:

HAL•LEONARD®
CORPORATION

7777 W. BLUEMOUND RD. P.O. BOX 13819 MILWAUKEE, WI 53213

Prices, contents and availability subject to change without notice.